Learning a Field Language

Learning a Field Language

Robbins Burling

The University of Michigan Press
Ann Arbor

LIBRARY OF CONGRESS CATALOGING IN PUBLICATION DATA

Burling, Robbins.
    Learning a field language.

    Includes bibliographical references.
    1. Language and languages—Study and teaching.
2. Anthropological linguistics—Field work.   I. Title.
P53.B87   1984   418′.007   84-11904
ISBN 0-472-08053-9 (pbk.)

Preface

My interest in language learning extends at least as far back as my own less than brilliant efforts to learn a language as a tool for conducting anthropological fieldwork. I did not learn very rapidly or very well when I was in the field, and I began to feel then, as I came to feel more insistently later, that anthropologists, as well as other field-workers whose interest in the language is more practical than theoretical, might use a rather different kind of guidance than had been most readily available.

The suggestions that I offer, therefore, are written first of all for field anthropologists who are not specialists in linguistics and who do not intend to make a systematic investigation of the language itself. Many others besides anthropologists find themselves traveling to distant places these days, however, and I hope my suggestions will be of interest to anyone who has the opportunity to live among those with a different language and who is willing to take personal initiative in devising ways to learn it. With the needs of such people in mind, both anthropologists and nonanthropologists, I have deliberately tried to keep my discussion of linguistic points as nontechnical as possible.

Discussions of linguistic field methods have usually come from linguists who have been more concerned with linguistic analysis and with investigating linguistic structure than is really necessary for most practical field-workers, but those who want more technical help than I offer here can turn to a number of sources for assistance. An old classic is Leonard Bloomfield's short *Outline Guide for the Practical Study of Foreign Languages* (Baltimore: Linguistic Society of America, 1942). Bloomfield offers some sage advice about how to elicit texts and take notes, but he is more concerned about describing how a language works than about offering practical steps for learning one. Another widely used classic is Sarah Gudschinsky's *How to Learn an Unwritten Language* (New York: Holt, Rinehart and Winston, 1967). Gudschinsky offers more advice about grammar and phonology than she does about vocabulary. She has some helpful things to say about the use of recordings, but she advocates transcribing them without worrying about their meaning. This, for practical purposes, I believe, puts the emphasis in precisely the wrong place.

Eugene Nida's *Learning a Foreign Language: A Handbook for Missionaries* (New York: National Council of Churches of Christ in the U.S.A., 1950), pays special attention to the linguistic requirements of bible translation and is considerably more technical than would be useful for most anthropologists. William J. Samarin's *Field Linguistics* (New York: Holt, Rinehart and Winston, 1967) contains lengthy discussions of social and personal factors in conducting fieldwork, and a detailed treatment of record keeping and methods of eliciting data. In spite of the hope for a broad audience that Samarin expresses in his introduction, however, his book is much more appropriate for a linguistic analyst than for a practical language learner. The most detailed guide that I am aware of, one that is directed especially to the language learner, is Alan Healey's *Language Learner's Field Guide* (Ukarumpa, Papua New Guinea: Institute of Linguistics,

1975), available in the United States through the Summer Institute of Linguistics. Healey's book offers a detailed sequence of steps to take in learning a language, and it emphasizes monolingual methods. I feel it has more on grammar and linguistic structure than is needed by most field-workers, other than linguists and translators, but like several of the works on learning a field language, it is written more with the needs of missionaries than anthropologists in mind. Field guides for anthropologists, such as Thomas Williams's *Field Methods in the Study of Culture* (New York: Holt, Rinehart and Winston, 1967), say very little about the practical steps in learning a language.

My suggestions are most directly relevant for those who wish to learn an unwritten language (or a language that has only recently been written) but who can, nevertheless, get some help from bilinguals who speak either English or another usable contact language. In two appendixes I offer brief notes about how my suggestions might be adapted to two somewhat different situations. The first appendix is intended for those who must learn their language without any contact language at all. The second is for those in the opposite situation and who wish to learn a more widely spoken or more literary language.

I would like to thank the Institutt for Sosialantropologi at the University of Oslo, Oslo, Norway, for offering me space and making me feel welcome while on leave from the University of Michigan. It was during my visit to Oslo that I did major work on the manuscript. I am also heavily indebted to good friends and colleagues, both in Oslo and in Ann Arbor, who have offered numerous trenchant criticisms of earlier drafts of the manuscript. I would like to thank, in particular, Eileen Cantrell, Even Hovdhaugen, Anne

Hvenekilde, Bruce Knauft, Thomas Moylan, and Aram Yengoyan as well as the remarkably thoughtful but anonymous reviewers recruited by the University of Michigan Press. Where I have failed to follow the advice of all these helpful people, it is my stubbornness rather than their good council that is to blame.

Contents

3 *Moving Ahead:*
Production

Notes

Appendixes

1 Background

Introduction

This book is intended for anyone who, like a field anthropologist, wants to learn a language in the field and is prepared to take personal initiative in deciding how to go about it. No two field situations are exactly alike, but I will have to make a number of assumptions about what you, as a learner, will want, and about what you will be able to do. I need to start by making these assumptions clear.

First, I will assume that you are more interested in language as a tool for communication than as an object to be investigated in its own right. I will assume that you will want to use the language in order to speak about all sorts of practical matters but that you will have no special or technical reason to explore its abstract structure. I will also assume that you will have few books either about, or in, the language that you want to learn. I will assume that you won't have grammatical descriptions and that you won't have dictionaries. Of course, such materials will sometimes be available, and when they are they can make your job easier. For the most part, however, I will write as if these aids do not exist. I will expect that you will be learning the language from those who speak it rather than from books. Without a trained teacher to guide you, you will have to decide for yourself what to do and how to do it.

In most of what I have to say, however, I will assume that you *will* be able to find people who know a certain amount of English or some other contact language that you can use, such as Spanish. (My use of the word *English,* from now on, should be understood as shorthand for "English or some other contact language.") I will assume that, either from kindness or because they like the wages that you pay, one or more people with some knowledge of English will be willing to help you. In Appendix 1, I offer some sketchy suggestions about the rare situation in which a learner has to manage without any common language at all, but even in the most remote parts of the world today, someone will most likely have been there before you and taught a few of the local people some English. Those who have learned a bit of the contact language are often delighted to practice their skills on a foreigner, and you will probably be able to entice one or more of them to help you with their language. So, realistically, let's assume that you will be able to find at least one person who can talk to you in a language that you already know. This person may not be very fluent and you may have to cope with all sorts of puzzling miscommunication even with someone who claims to "know" English, but you can probably get some important help.

You must realize, however, that being able to speak English is, at best, a mixed blessing. English is so important in the world today that you can almost always find someone to talk to. That can be a great comfort when far from home, but it can also tempt you to dispense entirely with the duty of learning another language yourself. Learning a language can be hard work, and there will be times when leaning on someone else to do your interpreting will seem like the easiest course to take. When people speak decent English it is awfully embarrassing to try to speak with them in broken Navajo or Tiv. You may have to fight against the temptation to resort too often to English, and if English is widely known in your area, you ought to make a regular effort to seek out the company of people who know no English. Anthropologists should keep reminding themselves that their job is to interpret one culture to another. To rely on a language interpreter is to turn over half the job to someone else. Anyone living among speakers of another language will find the experience vastly more rewarding if not restricted to English speakers. Nevertheless, in the beginning, English-speaking consultants can be an enormous help.

I will also assume that the language that you want to learn is too insignificant to be taught back home and that you will be unable to start its study before you reach the field. Finally, I will assume that you are sufficiently motivated, at the very start of your field trip, to make a substantial investment of time and energy working on the language. Learning a language is by no means a trivial chore. You need to be prepared not only for hard work, but for moments of dreadful discouragement. Communicating dimly through the veil of a poorly known language is both exhausting and frustrating. You have to be prepared to be laughed at, to be treated as an ignorant child. After several months you will probably still wonder if you have been wasting your time by indulging in the fantasy that it is even possible to learn that language.

On the other hand, language learning, especially in the field, is also likely to be one of the most exciting adventures that you ever undertake. As you gradually work your way into a better and better grasp of the language, you will also work your way into an ever better appreciation of the people who speak it and into a growing understanding of their culture. In the long run, the investment of a few months in learning a language will pay off handsomely. You will be able to learn far more in your second six months if you can speak directly with the people than you could hope to learn in a full year of seeing things murkily through the distortions of an interpreter. When you speak *their* language badly you will be constantly reminded of your misunderstandings. When you communicate through someone who speaks *your* language badly you may not even realize how much misunderstanding is being hidden from you.

The recommendations that I offer cannot be followed mechanically, like a recipe, and I do not think you can guide yourself into a new language with any efficiency unless you know what you are doing and why you are doing it. Each person also has his or her individual learning style, and so each person will have to adjust the techniques to suit personal preferences. For these reasons I will not be content with simply suggesting what I think you might try to do, but I will also take a good deal of space explaining the reasons for my suggestions. If you know something about the nature of language learning, you should be able to proceed on your own, creating your own techniques for learning that conform to your particular style and personality. This means that I have to take as much space to explain principles as to explain techniques.

Communication: The Exchange of Information
Above all, I want you to communicate. This means that I want you to understand others and to make yourself understandable to them. These sound like the obvious goals of

every language learner, but I think these simple goals need to be emphasized, because learners too often get diverted from them and fall into more of a struggle with the mechanics of grammar and pronunciation than they should. Learners can become timid about using what they know for fear of making horrible mistakes with what they don't know. All the attention paid to the mechanics of communication sometimes gets in the way of the communication itself. I will try to show you that it is possible to communicate a great deal with only a rudimentary speaking ability, if you can be unembarassed about mistakes, if you can be inventive with circumlocutions, and if you are willing to eke out your meager vocabulary with gestures.

If you really want to communicate, and not simply play at linguistic exercises, however, you will need to understand a great deal. You will, in fact, have to understand a far higher level of language than you will need to produce. When you speak, you can resort to gestures, synonyms, and circumlocutions, but the people with whom you will want to talk will not easily limit themselves to such a simple level.

The most successful language learners are often those who can get themselves into a situation where they can hear a vast amount of the language without being under pressure to speak. This is one of the reasons why grade school children are often so successful. They are allowed to sit and listen for several months with little direct pressure to talk. When they are ready, they sometimes begin to speak with astonishing suddenness.[1] As an adult, however, you may not be granted the privilege of waiting several months before needing to speak.

The amount of English that you will be able to use, or that you will want to use, depends upon the situation. When working in an area where a high proportion of the people know some English, as with American Indians for example, it may be embarrassing or even rude to attempt to speak in a broken tongue. Navajos or Senecas may be so accustomed to speaking English with outsiders that they find it difficult to use their own language. In extreme cases they may even find it an invasion of their privacy to have an outsider force his way into what they have regarded as their private language. One needs to reach an advanced level of linguistic skill before even being allowed to use it. In the face of such a dilemma, the best strategy is to work very hard on comprehension and postpone trying to say anything at all until you can understand a great deal. At the opposite extreme, it is still possible to find a few corners of the world where nobody knows any contact language at all. If you find yourself in such a remote spot, you will be forced, from the very first day, to struggle with speaking as well as with understanding. In such a case, you will have no choice.

Most field situations lie somewhere between these extremes. A few people may know some English, but most will not. You will then be able to fall back upon English in some situations, but you will certainly want to show your hosts that you are intent upon learning their language. Unless you start talking to them they are unlikely to talk much to you.

Nevertheless, in the pages that follow, I am going to emphasize techniques for learning to understand. I feel that this is the most neglected aspect of language pedagogy, and even if you find yourself in an area where little English is spoken, I am going to encourage you to work, just as quickly as possible, toward being able to understand the full, natural language, at its full, natural speed, as it comes tumbling from the lips of native speakers, even if this temporarily delays your own ability to speak. I want you to engage in conversation and, obviously, you cannot engage in conversation unless you say things yourself. I will, however, try to persuade you that you *can* hold up your end of the conversation using mushy pronunciation, rudimentary grammar, and a great many gestures. You will discover that improvement in speaking ability will come most easily as a by-product of your work on learning to understand.

In the early lessons of many language courses, students are encouraged to concentrate heavily upon pronunciation and grammar, while vocabulary is introduced only very slowly. The idea seems to be that even if one has very little to say, that little bit should be said correctly. Students may worry a great deal about the machinery of language, but they worry rather little about really communicating much of anything. Under such circumstances, learners have to think about an awful lot of things in order to construct even a simple sentence. They are supposed to force their mouths to produce sounds that seem ridiculous. They have to grope desperately for words that they barely know. They have to perform mental gymnastics trying to remember bizarre grammatical rules. All these challenges are a fatal distraction from what skillful speakers worry about—the message that they want to convey. If early learners have to worry about getting everything correct, they cannot hope to say anything very interesting. They simply cannot do everything at once and emerge with any real sense of success.

You learned your first language with no conscious awareness of its grammatical patterns. In some mysterious way you just soaked these patterns up. You may not even have realized that your first language had a grammar until you studied another language and discovered that it did not work like your mother tongue. Of course, you did learn the grammar of your native language, but you did it unconsciously, without paying attention.

We don't usually think it is possible to learn a second language (or a third or a ninth) in the same way that we learned our first language, and perhaps it is not. Perhaps adults are clever enough to take advantage of a certain amount of explicit grammar and thereby speed up the process. Adults don't really want to wait five years before reaching the kindergarten level, and a few grammatical rules may help to nudge things along faster. But I believe that most students of foreign languages are far too heavily burdened by explicit rules of grammar.

I don't think you have to learn your new language in just the same way that children learn their first language. You have different interests from a child and you don't have as much time. You can, for instance, use paper and pencil as a crutch for your memory. But it is possible to mimic a child's methods to some extent. If your understanding stays well in advance of your speaking ability (and be assured that it is possible to learn to understand a language fluently without ever saying anything at all), then the new forms that you gradually add to your active speech will already be familiar from comprehension. You will be able to draw upon long experience. You will have some sense of what sounds right. You may not be able to describe the grammatical patterns that make the language hang together, but that should make very little difference if your goal is to communicate.

Nevertheless, in most field situations, if you want to make a good impression on your hosts you will certainly want to say a few things from the very beginning. On your first day in the field, it is good to be able to use a few courtesy words, such as *hello, goodbye,* and *thank you,* or whatever it is that the people say in order to show that they are decently courteous human beings. This is simply part of adjusting to the local etiquette of polite behavior, and it goes along with learning the proper gestures and proper way of holding your body. As the weeks go by you will certainly try to say more and more, both for your own satisfaction and in order to demonstrate your progress to those among whom you are living. You will want your speaking to show steady improvement. Still, I want to persuade you to keep improving your comprehension even more rapidly.

Meaning and Grammar
One great advantage of an initial focus upon comprehension is that it concentrates your efforts squarely upon meaning. If you start by trying to understand, you will be forced, from the very beginning, to think about what the other person is trying to tell you. Meaning becomes central, and much of the grammar, including most of its fussiest and most annoying details, fades into the background. It is in this way that most people, most of the time, think about the relative importance of grammar and meaning. The reason you want to learn the language is so that you can communicate meaning. You will never get distracted from that goal as long as you concentrate upon understanding, and as long as you learn to talk in situations where you are really trying to get your meaning across rather than in situations where you simply practice mechanical drills.

When you focus on meaning, you inevitably focus also on

vocabulary, on words. You will have to try to figure out what words people are using and you will have to learn what their words mean. Of course you will need to hear the pronunciation clearly enough to distinguish the words from one another, but this is a relatively modest level of pronunciation skill and considerably less of a challenge than mouthing the words yourself. A certain rough-and-ready understanding of some aspects of grammar, such as favorite word order, will be helpful from the beginning, but if you understand enough words, you may be surprised at how much you can understand with only the most rudimentary grasp of the grammar.

Words, to be sure, cannot be totally separated from grammar. Not only does word order give information about how the words are related to one another, but the affixes that attach to words (including prefixes, suffixes, and even infixes), and the changes that the words themselves undergo in various circumstances (e.g., *foot/feet, go/went*), modulate the meanings of words in vital ways. In some languages the affixes that cluster around words or that fit inside them carry such crucial information that you will have to attend to them very early. Still, you can expect that the more important such affixes are, the more likely they are to be relatively stable and thus relatively easy to hear. Languages are not totally chaotic, and fixed sequences of sound do tend, more often than not, to convey consistent meanings. It is these sound sequences, usually words but occasionally affixes, that you want to learn to recognize.

Happily, it is these words, the consistent sequences of sound with consistent meaning, that the people with whom you will be dealing can most easily discuss. They will not be linguists and they will know little about the grammar of their language. They will very likely regard their pronunciation as simply the natural way to speak and be quite unable to understand the reasons for your amusing accent. They will, however, have no trouble telling you about their words. In our own highly literate society everyone uses dictionaries, and even in nonliterate societies people can isolate words and discuss them. They can point to things and name them and, even if they cannot read or write, they can explain and define their more abstract words. So by concentrating on comprehension you will inevitably focus on meaning, and this implies that you will also come to focus on vocabulary, the easiest part of the language for your new friends to explain.

Not all words, of course, are equally easy to talk about. Generally speaking, the nouns, verbs, and adjectives that refer to concrete, tangible phenomena (*child, run, hot,* etc.) are relatively easy to talk about and to learn. The grammatical particles, such as articles, prepositions, and the other little words that provide the matrix into which content words fit (*of, an, the, for, any,* etc.) are more difficult. These are known as "function words" and they join with affixes and with many kinds of word changes and word order changes to form the grammar of the language. Most people find their grammar much more difficult to talk about or to explain than their concrete content vocabulary. People use their function words consistently, just as they speak all aspects of their native language "grammatically," because it sounds right to do so, not because they can explain what they are doing. No one has much trouble defining (or demonstrating by pointing or gesturing) words like *girl, potato, black,* or *sleep,* but even fluent native speakers may find it impossibly difficult to define or explain the use of words like *the, for,* or *any,* or to explain why any of the grammatical patterns of their language must be followed.

It is an odd fact of language, however, that a great deal can be communicated with very little grammar. Telegraphic English and the language of newspaper headlines convey their messages primarily by content words. It is a graceless way to communicate, but it works. You will, of course, want to learn to understand, and eventually to use, the grammatical apparatus of the language, but if you do not insist on speaking with correct grammar too soon, you can avoid much of the difficulty that the grammar can otherwise cause. If you start with comprehension and if you learn to understand a great many content words, you will be able to get the gist of the message even with only a murky idea of why these content words come embedded in all that grammar.

As you listen to more and more of the language, however, you will get used to the grammar simply because its patterns repeat so regularly. The affixes and the function words that are most closely involved with the grammar will crop up over and over again, and their use will gradually come to seem natural. They will even begin to contribute something to the meaning. But just because they turn up so often, you should be able to soak up a good deal of the grammatical patterns by exposure, and you should not have to think about them as explicitly as you will have to think about the content words. You should not have to rely as heavily upon explanations of native speakers for the grammatical patterns or for the function words as you do for content words. This is a good thing, since you may not be able to get any clear explanations even if you try.

To insist upon correct grammar from the time you start to

speak imposes a painful and inhibiting responsibility. If you are patient at first, and not too puristic, you will be able to get a good deal of your meaning across with content words alone. If you aren't too proud, you can imitate Tarzan and say "Me no want water" instead of "I don't care for any water." They will understand.

Emphasizing comprehension at first should also ease your problems with pronunciation. By hearing a great deal of the language you will gain a solid sense of what it should sound like. When you talk, you should then be able to monitor your own pronunciation. By working on comprehension, therefore, you can reduce the problems that both pronunciation and grammar would otherwise cause. You will still have to struggle with vocabulary.

One of the snares of a good deal of recent language pedagogy has been the unspoken assumption that everything we know about language has to be taught. Linguists keep discovering wonderful new things about language, and every new discovery has been followed by ambitious pedagogical techniques for teaching it. The attempt is made to teach not only pronunciation, grammar, and vocabulary, but also intonation, communicative competence, turn taking, performance, etc. I am offering quite different advice. I am saying that a language is far too complex to be learned all at once, and I think a beginner should concentrate on the essentials. At first, I don't think you need to worry very much about pronunciation or even about grammar. Speaking beautifully will be well beyond your grasp for a while and you shouldn't feel that you have to try. I think you will make the most rapid progress if you focus your effort on learning to understand, just as quickly as you can, as many content words as possible.

I am convinced that the real challenge in learning a language is to learn to recognize and to understand all that vocabulary. People know tens of thousands of words in their native language. You may never master that many words in your new language, but if you are to communicate with any ease you will certainly have to recognize many thousands. You don't really need to produce so many in order to make yourself understood, but even learning to understand most of the words that other people use can be a daunting challenge. Anything you can do to minimize the time spent on other aspects of the language will leave more energy for this most essential task. If, at first, you focus your energies on learning to recognize and to understand words, and if you avoid worrying too much about being able to recall them, you will be able to conquer vocabulary at a much faster rate. Then, as you come to understand easily an increasing number of words, it should not be too difficult to convert the most essential of these words to active use.

Mnemonics

When I was in the first or second grade I had trouble remembering how to spell certain words, and I devised some tricks to help myself. The only tricks that I still remember are: "There are too many *o*'s in *too*," and "There are two points on one of the letters in *two*." I was careful never to tell anyone about my memory tricks because I had already absorbed the popular wisdom that there was something sneaky about them. I thought I was cheating. I thought I was supposed to rely on some sort of "pure" memory. Now, however, I look back upon my tricks as rather clever devices for a grade school child to have devised, and I wish I had been encouraged to use such tricks when memorization was unavoidable.

Rote memory used to be more respectable than it is today. American children once memorized not only the multiplication tables, but also the state capitals and the order of the presidents, to say nothing of great lists of dates. Nobody felt that this was an infringement upon basic freedoms. In modern American education, however, memory has fallen upon hard times. We want our students to understand, to see the meaning of things, to synthesize and abstract.

If you want to learn a language, however, you have to memorize, and if you want to learn a language quickly, you have to memorize efficiently. You will, in particular, be able to speed things up if you take deliberate steps to memorize vocabulary. You will not have all the years of childhood in which to absorb those thousands of words. The faster you can learn to understand words, the better off you will be. In this section I am going to teach you a trick to help you to recall the meaning of words when you hear them. At first, this trick may strike you as silly, but I urge you to give it a fair chance. I thought it was silly when I first heard it too, but when I tried it and found that it actually doubled the rate at which I could learn to recognize words, I became angry with all my language teachers for their failure to teach me the trick much earlier. Since words form such a major part of the challenge of language learning, anything that increases the speed of acquiring words will increase the overall rate of progress by almost the same proportion.

The trick is called the "Keyword" method.[2] When you want to learn a word in your new language, you must think of a word in your *own* language that sounds or looks a bit like the word you are trying to learn. If, for instance, you are trying to learn the French word *champs* 'field' you will probably think of the colloquial English abbreviation for *champions*. This word from your own language is the Keyword, and it need have no connection at all, or any meaning in common, with the word you are trying to learn. In fact, the method seems to work best if the new foreign word and the Keyword have nothing in common except for their sound or appearance.

Next, you should dream up some association between the meaning of the English Keyword and the meaning of the word you want to learn. Construct some image—the sillier the better—that connects the two meanings. You might think of some champs, flexing their impressive muscles while standing in a field. The next time you run into the French word, you think, "Ha, *champs*. What did I think of 'champs' doing? Oh, yes. They are standing in a 'meadow' or some such place. That must be the meaning of the French word *champs.*" One of the advantages of the Keyword method is that you remember in images instead of by means of an English word. When you first get a translation of *champs* it may be the word *field,* but by remembering an image of a grassy place rather than a particular English word, you soon become emancipated from your own language.

I wanted to remember the meanings of the words for the four seasons in Chinese: *syàtyān* 'summer', *chyōutyān* 'fall', *dūngtyān* 'winter', and *chwūntyān* 'spring'. The *tyān* appears in all four words so it does nothing to distinguish them, and I had to focus primarily on the first syllable. Sometimes it is unnecessary to include all of the foreign word in the sound-alike Keyword, so I thought that the *yat* in *syàtyān* sounded like a nice boat that people might use in the summertime.

For fall, I remembered the name of Choate, a New England prep school, and I thought of its buildings surrounded with the colored leaves of fall. I had to stretch my imagination for *chwūntyān* but then thought that in spring "each one" turns to thoughts of love. Winter was easy. I simply thought of something that a dog had left behind in the snow. The associations are absurd, but I suspect that if you look back on these four Chinese words now, you will be much more likely to remember which is which than you would have been without the help of these associations.

The Keyword method, to be sure, works better with words for concrete visible objects than for more abstract words, but concrete words are *always* easier to remember, and the Keyword method is by no means useless for even the most abstract of terms. At times it is difficult to find an English word or phrase that sounds anything at all like the exotic sequence of sounds of the foreign word, but with enough ingenuity something can usually be dredged up. How do you remember that the Swedish word *invecklad* means *complicated?* You might realize that it would be very complicated to get anything done if you had to put your confidence "in a weak lad." Farfetched? Of course, but that doesn't matter if it helps you to remember what *invecklad* means.

The Keyword method is better adapted for helping you to remember the meaning of a foreign word when you encounter it ("foreign-to-meaning" direction) than for helping you to remember a foreign word when you are trying to talk, and this means that it is best adapted to the comprehension-first approach. When you start to memorize vocabulary you may sometimes be tempted to start with an English word and try to remember a foreign equivalent ("English-to-foreign" direction). Think, for instance, of flash cards with an English word on one side and a corresponding foreign word on the other. You can look first at either side and try to remember what is on the other side. I do *not* recommend that you make yourself a lot of flash cards, but thinking about them makes the difference between the foreign-to-meaning and the English-to-foreign directions obvious, and I want to urge you strongly, certainly during your first months in the field, always to work in the foreign-to-meaning direction. It is this direction to which the Keyword method is best adapted.

Listen to, write down, and look at the words in your new language that you hear in conversation, and exert your memory so that you can recall their meaning. Memorizing in that direction is much easier than trying to remember foreign equivalents of English words. You can acquire words at a much faster rate that way, for you will not have to fix every detail of the foreign word in your head as you would if you needed to recall it. You merely need to recognize it.

This will, to be sure, leave you groping for words when you try to say something yourself, but there is really nothing that can save you from this groping. You may imagine that forcing yourself to memorize in the English-to-foreign direction will enable you to find the right words when you try to talk, but it is more likely to foster a kind of garbled and overly literal translation from English. Memorizing in the English-to-foreign direction also keeps you tied to English at a time when you should be freeing yourself from your own language and orienting yourself in your new one. It is better to be patient and let the words that you learn to recognize become consolidated by hearing them repeatedly in genuine contexts. You will then find yourself able to use the words yourself, not as translations from English, but in the places where they really belong. The Keyword method can be a great help in achieving this goal.

Why does the Keyword method work? Perhaps it is only because it focuses your attention on the word and makes you think about it, and because it gives you positive steps to take as you try to remember it. But I think there is more to it than just the focusing of attention. The method seems to exploit something about the way our memory works. You will find that you remember the meaning of your new words in images, rather than by means of verbal equivalents in English. Far from tying you to English, which might seem to be its danger, the Keyword method actually seems to emancipate you from English. It is a remarkably effective, yet very simple trick.

You may learn to recognize some words so easily that constructing the images required by the Keyword method would be a waste of energy. Some words, such as names for concrete tangible objects, and especially the names of objects that have no obvious equivalent in your own language, may be absorbed with little or no effort. But as soon as you notice words cropping up whose meaning you keep forgetting, it is time to try mnemonic tricks. The Keyword method is one such trick, but you may find others. Just remember: there is no virtue at all in brute force memory. Use your ingenuity to devise associations and tricks that will help you to understand words just as quickly as possible.

Reading and Oral Comprehension

I assume that your goal is to use the spoken language. In some cases you will have reading as a secondary goal, but the point of a field language is to understand and to produce its spoken form. Nevertheless, some of the problems that you will face in the field will be clarified if you think, for a bit, of the differences between learning to read and learning to understand a spoken language. In spite of the great emphasis that recent language pedagogy has placed upon the spoken language, classroom instruction is often most successful at teaching people to read. Students who are very good readers sometimes find themselves quite baffled when they go to a foreign country for the first time and find themselves lost in the torrent of words that comes rushing at them. The problems of learning a spoken language may be clarified if we understand why reading so often comes more easily. There are, I think, at least four reasons.

First, as a reader you set your own pace. You can read as slowly as you want and you can go back repeatedly over a passage until you figure it out. When you listen to the spoken language the other fellow sets the pace and it may be much too fast to manage.

Second, words in print are far more stable than they are in speech. We alter the pronunciation of our spoken words according to the context in which they are found and according to our mood and degree of relaxation. When speaking very carefully we can say "I am going to go" but more often we are satisfied with "I'm gonna go" or "Ahmunu go" or "Ahmugo." We can say "What are you doing?" or "Wachadoin?" Almost everything we say can be reduced, collapsed, abbreviated, and this means that every word has several alternative pronunciations. When we know a language well, we take these alternations and contractions for granted. We are not even surprised that the spelling of words remains stable in spite of their varied pronunciations.

But when we struggle to understand someone who is speaking naturally, but in a language we know poorly, we can be totally mystified by his phonological abbreviations.

Third, the spoken language has a good many words (perhaps *noises* is a better term) that carry important meaning but that practically never find their way into print. I am not thinking here of tabooed words such as obscenities and blasphemies, although these do pose problems for foreigners, but of things like "ohoh," "unhunh," and "oops." Noises such as these are very common, and they have to be understood easily by anyone desiring a comfortable ability to understand. Books provide very little practice with them.

Finally, modern written languages come with their words all nicely set off by white spaces fore and aft. When the words are unfamiliar, it is even possible to look them up in a dictionary. In spoken language the words are all messily run together, and you may even find it hard to know where one word ends and the next begins, let alone figure out what they all mean. If you can't even figure out what the words are, you can't ask someone for their meanings, and you certainly can't look them up in a dictionary. Often they just fly by too quickly to grab.

These special problems of the spoken language explain why going to the movies or listening to the radio is not a very effective way of learning a foreign language. Things go by too quickly and there is simply no way to "look things up" when you don't understand. Movies and the radio cannot be the spoken equivalent of a book. You can't set your own pace and it is very difficult to find the meaning of an unknown word.

If your goal is to learn the spoken language, you need to find ways of overcoming these special problems. Fortunately, the spoken language is easier than reading in at least two compensating ways, its vocabulary range and the support of the nonverbal context.

First, the vocabulary of spoken language tends to be much more repetitious. In an extensive word count of typical written English, it was found that the most common 8,000 words made up about 90 percent of the running vocabulary. In a comparable sample of spoken English, 90 percent of the vocabulary was accounted for by only about 800 words, only one-tenth as many.[3] Of course, several thousand of the words that make up the remaining 10 percent will also have to be learned, but the vocabulary range of spoken language does present a less formidable challenge than that of written language. One who is interested primarily in the spoken language can probably avoid, at least for a while, some of the fancier literary vocabulary that people use in writing. Anyone who wants to read a literary language will need many more words.

Second, the spoken language is always embedded in a rich nonverbal context and accompanied by gestures, emphasis, and tone of voice, all of which help the listener to sort out the meaning. A vast amount of our communication system is never represented in writing at all. In fact, when we write, we have to compensate for these missing features of our spoken language. This is one reason why writing is different from speech. When you learn to understand oral language you can make use of the gestures and emphasis that accompany speech and you can use all the cues of the nonverbal context. This should make oral comprehension much easier.

Your problems in learning to understand, therefore, come down to learning to recognize a large number of words (but far less, at first, than you would need for reading), and to recognize them instantaneously and in all their varied spoken forms. You have to learn to exploit whatever advantages the spoken language offers and to overcome its special difficulties.

Full-Time Study

It has been the experience of language teachers that, when students are sufficiently well motivated, the more hours per day that their students spend studying language, the more they will learn in each hour.[4] In other words, students will learn more in one week of study at eight hours per day than they will learn in eight weeks of study at one hour per day, even though the total number of study hours is the same. It may be that people learn more quickly if they are able to build on what they have learned in the previous lessons before they have a chance to forget it. The nearly full-time nature of their exposure to language is one reason why children sometimes seem to learn languages so rapidly when taken to another country. They are often immersed for many hours every day in the new language while their parents spend much of their time speaking their mother tongue. Different concentrations of exposure also help to explain why immersion programs tend to be relatively successful, and why high school and college classes that meet only for a few hours each week make such dismally slow progress.

The conclusion seems obvious. If you want to learn a field language, the only sensible thing to do is to work at it full time when you first get to the field. Don't imagine that you are going to accomplish much else for a while. Simply by learning the language, of course, you will also be learning a good deal about the people and their culture, but you might resist the temptation to tell yourself, "I've worked on the language enough for a while and I can't afford more time. I will use an interpreter temporarily and get some real work done." Interrupting your language study may, in the long run, force you to spend more total time on the language than if you did nothing, at first, except language study. So I urge you to concentrate on the language. Once you have a good start, you will be able to do other things far more easily and have far more fun doing them. In the rest of what I have to say, therefore, I will assume that you will be willing to work full time on the language for the first few months of your stay in the field. Of course, as you practice the language you will be talking about what is going on around you and you will want to keep your ears wide open. You will surely learn a good deal about your surroundings. Still, you will inevitably face frustrations. You will not learn as fast as you think you should. Occasionally you will wonder if the effort is even worth it. Hang in there. It is.

Equipment

In addition to some file cards and plenty of paper and pencils, I suggest that you take one piece of equipment with you to the field: a good tape recorder. You will want to be able to run it on batteries, and a binaural recorder with binaural earphones for play back will help you to sort out voices more easily than if you have only a single-track recorder. Microphones that you can hang around people's necks are best. It may also be helpful if your recorder has a variable-speed playback control.

2 Starting Out: Comprehension

In the Field

You have reached the field. You have a place to live and some sort of food in your belly. Now what?

You hear the language swirling about you, but it goes by too fast to be of much use. You can point to things and get their names, but there is more to a language than names for visible objects. Sometimes people will want to talk with you and then they will take the initiative themselves. You should welcome these occasions but you will probably find it exhausting to try to answer questions that you hardly understand in a language that you barely control, and after a while the others will also get tired and bored. It will be hard work for them to struggle with broken communication, just as it is hard work for you. You should try to capitalize on any chance encounters with the language that happen to come your way. Notice what people say, and jot down any words that you think you understand. But you cannot just sit back and wait. You will probably want to take some initiative and devise some deliberate strategies.

Things will go faster if you find individuals who are willing to help you by acting as "consultants." If at least one of them knows some English, you will be able to take some shortcuts. The obvious and probably inevitable way to start is to ask for translations of words and phrases from English that you think would be useful to know. You can ask how to say *house, moon, That is a pretty cloth, What do you call that in your language?*, *Please speak more slowly,* or *Would you like a cup of tea?* if those seem to be important things to learn. But you run one serious risk if you do too much of this or if you practice your new phrases too carefully with a consultant who is specifically employed to help you. A conscientious consultant may feel obliged to correct every error you make. This soon becomes depressing and counterproductive. It forces you to think about how you are saying things instead of about what you are saying. I feel that you can get more useful practice with speaking when you are in less formal situations, in which people are interested more in what you say than in how you say it. These are likely to be situations in which people will coax you, and encourage you to make your meaning clear, and in which they will tolerantly ignore your garbling of their language. There certainly will be times when, in speaking casually with people, you find yourself needing, sometimes desperately, a way of expressing some meaning. It is sensible to keep track of these so that you can ask your English-speaking consultant the next time you meet, but for the most part the time spent with specifically employed consultants is, I feel, much better spent on comprehension.

Explain that you want to practice understanding and solicit their cooperation. You can ask consultants to point to things of their own choosing and to name them. Then have them ask you such questions, in their language, as "Is this an *X*?" You can answer with a nod or a shake of the head (or whatever equivalent gestures are used where you are living), and this will give you practice understanding the words without being forced to say them yourself. Your consultants should be able to get the idea that you want them to ask questions that will sometimes require a *yes* for an answer and sometimes a *no.* Sometimes they will point to their own nose and ask, "Is this my eye?" and you had better answer "No." They can also ask about *your eye* and *my eye* and thereby teach you to recognize possessive pronouns. They can ask questions about manipulable objects. *Is this a piece of paper? Is the pencil on top of the paper? Is the paper green? Am I sitting on a chair? Is there a window in this house?* They can also tell you to do things and you can demonstrate your understanding by obeying. *Pick up the pencil. Walk over to the door. Give me two pieces of paper.* With a certain amount of cooperative ingenuity, you can build up quite rapidly to rather complex but still understandable sentences.[5]

Proceeding in this way, you should be able to move steadily ahead. At first you will have to concentrate hard on the major content words so as to ferret out the meaning of what you hear. You may discover that you can understand a good many sentences without being sure how you understand them. Words that you can recognize (*eye, nose, my, your, pencil, chair, green, big, sit, walk,* etc.) will come to you decorated with a grammatical apparatus, the exact nature of which may be murky at first, but as long as you understand the overall meaning of what your consultants say, you needn't worry about the details.

Of course you can ask your consultants to explain the meaning of the grammatical markers that you hear, such as affixes and function words, but don't be dismayed if their answers are sometimes confusing, misleading, or simply wrong. Most people have only a dim idea of how the grammar of their language works. Think of how badly an English speaker might cope with a request to explain the meaning of *the, any,* or *-ing.* This does not mean that you shouldn't ask. Indeed you should ask, because sometimes you will get clear and useful answers. But when their answers are murky, be content with the general meaning of the sentences that you hear. The subtleties can wait. In the meantime your sense of how the language is built will grow with every new sentence.

Your comprehension will improve most rapidly if you do not get distracted by trying to produce the language with correct grammar and pronunciation. When you work on comprehension you have to listen carefully, for words will come at you very fast. Now and then words that your consultant insists are different will sound very much alike. Nevertheless, it will be easier to hear what is important than to reproduce the sounds yourself. Nor does grammar pose problems as difficult for a listener as for a speaker. When listening, you will notice that the meaningful elements you begin to recognize sometimes come in an unfamiliar order and they may change in surprising ways from one sentence to another, but neither pronunciation nor grammar will be your main obstacle. When listening, it will be vocabulary, the speed with which you can learn to recognize words as they come tumbling from the lips of your consultants and friends, that will be the chief limitation to your progress.

You learned your native language without the help of writing, and with enough time and patience you could probably learn another language in the same way. A literate person can speed things up by taking notes, however, so when you hear a new word in a context that leads you to believe that you know what it means (or when you have what seems to be a reliable translation) jot it down on paper with a rough

English equivalent. Spell it as best you can. Use familiar letters for familiar sounds and make up symbols for unfamiliar sounds. You will help yourself if you are reasonably consistent and if you try always to use the same symbol for the same sound. However, if you think of your notes not as precise transcriptions, but simply as a means for triggering off memories of what you have heard, then the particular spelling you choose will not be so important at this stage. As your consultants speak, you can try to memorize the meanings of as many words as possible, but if you keep the words on a list you can also use moments of quiet and solitude (if your field situation allows such a luxury) to work on them some more and commit them to memory.

A handy list of common words and ten minutes of attention to them from time to time should speed things up, but I would advise against flash cards. They too easily encourage long frustrating bouts of brute memory. The words on flash cards are deprived of any real context, and it is easy to let flash cards trap you into imagining that the words in your new language are simple equivalents of English words, rather than independent words that stand for their own concepts.

Remember the Keyword method, or devise other mnemonic tricks. Use these tricks to speed up the recognition of words and to avoid brute force memory. Use some common sense, however. Don't waste energy on words you suspect to be very rare, or on grammatical particles whose meanings are, at first, obscure. Particles and other function words will reappear with very high frequency, and you will gradually get used to hearing them in the right places. That is probably the most strategic way to learn them.

For most languages today, even inconspicuous ones, you will be able to find some sort of word list or small dictionary. If a list or dictionary is available, by all means use it. Even a short word list can save you much time and effort by leading you quickly to the most common words. If you cannot find any sort of word list at all, it will probably be worthwhile to build up a file. Whenever you encounter a new word that seems worth learning, put it on a separate card (such as an index card) along with a translation. File the cards in alphabetical order by word, not by translation. Then, when you hear a word that you know you have heard before, but whose meaning you cannot recall, you will have a fighting chance of finding it in your file. Unless you want to make out two cards for each word and keep two separate files, *don't* file the words by the English translations. Your first job is to learn to recognize foreign words, not to recall them, so the file should be arranged in a way that will allow you to start with your new language.

You will want your consultants to give you sentences that contain useful words, but it is better to have them make up their own sentences than to ask them to translate English sentences that you supply. Their own sentences are more likely to be formed according to the natural patterns of the language. This will also keep it clear that you are working on comprehension. It may help, however, if you keep in mind a sort of checklist of semantic areas for which you would like to learn some vocabulary and for some of these you can elicit words by pointing or acting out. Here are some examples of areas that are appropriate for your checklist.

The easiest area of all, except that it includes an endless number of words, is the naming of concrete objects—body parts, small manipulable objects, buildings and their parts, clothing, natural objects of the earth, sea, and sky, foods, plants, animals, people, etc. There are words (very likely verbs) for simple activities: *sit, stand, go, come, talk, sleep, eat*. There are also words for qualities. These are usually adjectives in English, but in other languages the words that describe color, shape, or size are sometimes either nouns or verbs. You can learn far more of these words by concentrating on learning to recognize them, rather than by laboring to recall them for active use. Of course, they will sometimes pop into your mind without special effort, and then you can have the joy of using them, but you don't need to force the issue.

One group of words, generally including some prepositions (or, in some languages, *postpositions*) as well as some adverbs and demonstratives, indicate position in space. These are relatively easy to elicit since you and your consultant can manipulate objects and discuss what is on top of, below, next to, or inside of what. Words for time are more difficult to derive from the immediate surroundings, but you can get your consultant to teach you to understand words for *morning, yesterday, later, earlier,* etc. You will also want words for quantity, including numbers, and whenever a question word, such as *who, what,* or *when,* turns up, grab it. Challenge your consultants to devise ways of teaching you to understand the words that they find important in all these domains. Remember, of course, that the words that are important vary from culture to culture. Not only do some people find a word for *yams* to be more important than a word for *bread*, but some find little use for *yellow* or *five*. You want to learn the words that *they* find important.

In addition to relatively concrete words (generally nouns, verbs, and adjectives), you will encounter a large number of function words. You may find these words more difficult to learn than the more concrete content words, but some of them will be very common and they do contribute in important ways to the meaning. Learn to recognize as many of these function words as you can. They will ease comprehension. A detailed classification of function words is not likely to be of much help while you are focusing upon comprehension. You must simply do your best to learn to recognize those that crop up. As you start to speak more actively, you may find the categories listed in the next chapter in the section entitled "The Functional Vocabulary" to be helpful.

Unless you are working among people where English is so widespread that it makes you shy about using the new language, you will surely want to supplement your systematic study with less formal conversation. Visit with people, including monolinguals, under many circumstances. Such occasions offer the most useful practice with speaking and allow a growing, receptive knowledge to be readily converted to productive use. It is then that both you and the people you are speaking with will be focusing on meaning while remaining unconcerned with grammatical niceties.

Of course, you can use times of informal conversation as occasions for improving your comprehension as well. If people can see that you are making progress with their language, they may find it fun to point to things and tell you their names. Jot these words down. Speakers will often embed their words in phrases, simply because that is the way people use language, and it is likely to be quite artificial to use single words all by themselves. Instead of pointing to an object and saying "tree" they may say "That is a tree." If you can figure out from the context what those extra noises mean, jot them down too. At least make a guess. You are engaged in solving a very complex puzzle, and you want to keep listening and noticing and guessing.

For a good many weeks and months, the casual and connected conversations that you hear others using when
speaking to one another will be too fast to be accessible, but
people do use some words and short phrases in isolation.
Listen for what people say when they stub their toe or when
they shout at a baby not to get too close to the fire. Listen
for what they say when they meet one another and when
they separate—their greetings and farewells. You will get a
feeling for the overall patterns of communication if you
learn to understand such things. The more of these phrases
you come to understand, the better you will be tuned in.

You may find one or two people who are particularly helpful and particularly clever at devising ways of instructing you.
Some people are good at simplifying their language and you
will, inevitably, enjoy the company of some more than
others. You might guard against relying too much on too few
people, however. Working with several people reduces the
burden of fatigue on any single individual and also reduces
the risk of being misled by one or two people's idiosyncra-
sies. If you spend too much time with a single individual, that
person may even develop special ways of addressing you. A
single individual can, quite inadvertently, cut you off from
the more natural language that other people use. It helps to
have at least one consultant who knows some of your language, but if other people get the idea of what you want, they
will be able to help you too. Monolinguals are perfectly capable of constructing simple sentences for you to practice
with, and speaking with monolinguals has the great advantage of forcing you to leave English behind.

It can be especially useful to practice with children. Children may find it intriguing to figure out ways of helping you
to understand, and you are likely to be relatively unself-

conscious about your own linguistic deficiencies when speaking with them. You can probably also be confident that when children get bored they will quit. You don't have to worry about imposing upon their goodwill. You can also be quite confident that children will give you the natural language and not an artificial version that they imagine will be easier for a foreigner.

The amount of time that you can spend with consultants or in free conversation with others will be limited by your pocketbook, by your endurance, and by their patience. Before too many hours are up, one of you will have had enough. You will want useful ways to work on the language when you are alone. The lists of words and phrases that you collect will demand some attention, but by some judicious recording of what they say, you can make your time with consultants more valuable. You can then go back and review what you have heard. It is helpful to listen several times, drilling the words and sentences into your head.

Recordings, however, are tricky to use. If they are too difficult they are almost useless. You can listen repeatedly without having any means of figuring out what was said. If recordings are too easy, on the other hand, you will find yourself reviewing things that you already know and for which no review is necessary. What you need is something of intermediate difficulty, something that is challenging but that you can still figure out, something that you don't easily understand at first but that you can learn to understand with some work.

Turn on your tape recorder when a consultant is producing challenging sentences. Later, you can listen to the sentences, trying to understand them but turning to your notes and your word collection when you need help. Hearing these sentences repeated a number of times will help to fix the grammatical and phonological patterns, as well as the vocabulary, in your mind. You can multiply the value of an hour or two with a consultant if you can spend another hour or two listening to what was said. Don't, however, imagine that you can record everything. A five-minute recording can easily deserve an hour of listening. An hour of recording will probably be quite useless. Be selective and get five good minutes that deserve close attention, and avoid useless longer passages.

If you work concertedly on learning to understand, sometimes sitting with a consultant whom you hire to help you and who will follow your instructions, sometimes accepting the help of adults or children who are willing to talk to you more casually, sometimes concentrating on the spontaneous conversations that swirl about you, sometimes working alone with recordings and notes, your ability should steadily improve. Your consultants and friends should be able to lead you into more and more complex levels of the language. By working many hours each day, you should be able to consolidate what you learn into your permanent memory before you have a chance to forget. But don't expect to understand two other people in rapid conversation just yet. That will take more time.

Connected Language

One of the major challenges that you will face will be rapid speech. The words and isolated sentences with which you are compelled to begin cannot give you adequate practice with the abbreviated phonology of high-speed language. You need experience with fast, natural speech since that is what you must finally understand, but the ordinary conversation that rushes around you will, at first, seem far beyond your capabilities. You will have no obvious way of breaking into it. You need some stepping-stones.

One technique is to record passages longer than a single sentence. You are not likely to find longer passages useful until you can recognize several hundred of the most common words, for only then will a high enough proportion of the words in a passage be understood, to allow the rest to become accessible. The general sentence patterns of the language, including, at a minimum, the dominant word order, should also seem at least vaguely familiar. You may still feel shaky about the meaning of a good many of the grammatical particles, but these should at least begin to sound familiar. Once you have reached this level, it may be time to try connected passages.

Ask one of your consultants to talk briefly on some subject that comes easily to her. She might describe the local houses, or she might tell you about the members of her family and how they are related to each other, or she might recount a recent incident. Myths are occasionally helpful because they are often quite repetitious, but myths are sometimes recited in a style so different from daily speech as to cause more confusion than help. You don't want your consultant to talk about something too far out of the ordinary, because it is the ordinary daily vocabulary that you want. You also don't want to let her talk too long. A mere five minutes can easily produce between 500 and 1,000 words, and even if you already know 90 percent of them, you will still be left with plenty of unknowns.

You should encourage your consultant to speak at a natural speed when you make the recordings. This is the speed you will need to understand, and it does little good to practice with artificially slow speech. One thing you will soon discover, however, is that many words you thought you knew will be pronounced in very abbreviated fashion. As soon as people speak naturally they begin to slough off some sounds. Artificial sentences produced in isolation provide very poor practice with such rapid speech, but if you are going to learn to understand real conversations, it is this kind of speech that you must practice with. You may as well get used to it.

Once you have a few minutes on tape, go over the passage, phrase by phrase, with your consultant. Whenever you come to a word that you do not recognize, ask your consultant for its meaning and make a note. (Clearly this is one place where a consultant who knows some English can be a great help.) As before, there will be affixes, grammatical particles, and function words for which your consultant may have trouble supplying a clear meaning or explanation. Do not press her to do what she cannot do, but when the meanings of these grammatical bits and pieces are clear, be careful to note them. If your consultant cannot explain some affix or function word, and if you cannot figure it out, be content with the general meaning of the sentence.

When you listen to your recording you will hear little bits and blips of sound that you can hardly recognize as speech, but that your consultant will identify as entire words or even phrases. Believe her. She knows her language. All you can do is accept what she tells you, just as someone else would have to accept your assurances that "wachadoin" really does mean "What are you doing?" A major part of your job will be to get a sense of this kind of abbreviated speech. Listening to recordings of fast speech is a good way to build up this sense, as long as you know what the recordings are supposed to mean. If you don't get somebody to help you, it may take a very long time to puzzle through these passages, but if you can get people to tell you what the noises stand for, you will begin to build up a sense for the sounds until they finally seem as natural to you as to them. That is when you will start to know the language.

If you have a variable speed tape recorder, it may help, when you are first trying to understand a passage, to turn down the speed just slightly. You cannot slow it down very far or you will get too much distortion of pitch and the sound will be very unnatural, but a slight slowing down may give just enough extra time to let you understand. You can speed it up on the next listening so as to become accustomed to natural speed.

Your goal with these recordings should be to listen to them straight through and to be able to understand everything without looking at your notes. To do this you will have to be able to understand the words quickly and easily, almost intuitively. Natural speech is so fast that you will have no time to think things out. You will not have the time to puzzle through the grammar or to worry about details of pronunciation. You will certainly not have time to translate what you hear into English. You will have to understand the message directly. Unlike reading, you cannot set your own pace. You have to follow along at natural speed.

Even a very short passage of three or four minutes is likely to give you considerably more natural speech than the isolated sentences that either you or your consultant make up. You will hear sentences constructed as they should be constructed and related to each other in natural ways. You will get the kinds of grammatical particles that people are really likely to use. You will get hesitations, false starts, and clearings of the throat—all things that you will need to cope with. And of course you will get lots of vocabulary.

Although there is wide variation from one passage to another, a five-minute sample of spoken colloquial language can have a total of 800 or so words. Because of repetitions there may be no more than 300 different words in such a passage, but even if you have learned several hundred words before you start to work on short samples of connected speech, you can be confident that plenty of new words will turn up in any natural sample. Learn to recognize any of the new words that you suspect to be common enough to make memorization worthwhile.

Record a short passage, go over it carefully with your consultant, and then work on it later in the day until you feel content with your ability to understand it. The next day, record another passage and handle it the same way. As your recognition vocabulary grows, and as you become accustomed to some of the variability that words show from one sentence to the next and from one passage to the next, you should be able to handle somewhat longer passages. Each passage will offer new words that are worth learning. With each, you will grow a bit more familiar with the pronunciation and grammatical patterns. Slowly you will even find that some of the grammatical patterns begin to make sense. You will then be able to use your growing sense of the grammar to help untangle the meaning.

If you look for topics that interest your consultant, you can also learn something about the culture of the people. You can ask for descriptions of various aspects of their technology and social organization and, as you learn to understand more easily, you can ask your consultants to branch out to increasingly abstract aspects of the culture. While you are doing all of this, of course, you should continue to do other things. Listen to others talking. Note the patterns of their dialogues. Listen to see if you can hear the same things from all speakers that you hear from your primary consultants. You will sometimes want to produce the language yourself and to try, gradually, to extend your ability to talk, but I think it is still a mistake to force it. When you talk, you should be able to base your talking on what you have often heard. It is through hearing that you will gain a sense of the best way to say things.

Conversation

I have recommended that you start by learning to understand words and sentences and then move on to short monologues, but even monologues fall short of a fully natural use of language. The most common use to which language is put is in conversation among two or more people, and this conversational exchange is your real goal. You need to be able to understand the rapid conversation of others, and you need to be able to participate in conversations yourself. You will be able to participate with a relatively rudimentary speaking ability, but the people you talk to cannot be trusted to answer at an equivalently rudimentary level. You have to be prepared to understand anything that they say.

Your next step, therefore, might be to record two people in conversation, but you will run into serious difficulties if you try to record genuine unstaged talk. People don't sit in places that are convenient to the microphone, they turn their heads, or the background noise masks what they say.

Eventually you should try to get some natural conversations but it will be much easier to start with staged ones. Obviously, you will need at least two helpers.

By the time you try this, you should have some idea, even if it is not yet precise, about a few of the normal topics of conversation in your community, or about some of the social situations that call for talk. What do people say when they meet on the road? How do people bargain over the price of cloth at the market? How do people ask directions to the spot with the best wild bamboo shoots? How do a husband and wife plan their day's activities? How do people invite others to a feast? What are the negotiations that lead up to an agreement of marriage? Ask your consultants to act out short sequences, each playing a different role. Set the general topic, but don't have them rehearse. By the time you ask people to help you in this way, you will have some sense of how long a passage you can handle, but it isn't likely to be very long just yet.

As before, as soon as you have recorded such a conversation, sit down with your consultants and go over the recording carefully. Ask for explanations of any words, phrases, or sentences that you do not understand. A conversation between two people is likely to be a good deal more difficult to understand than a monologue. You will have to cope with a number of new problems: questions and answers, signals for turn taking, interruptions, and overlaps. Simply because two (or more) people are participating, a conversation is rarely as clearly planned ahead of time as a monologue, and there are likely to be more broken sentences and false starts. These are all things you will need practice with, however. Listen to your recorded conversations repeatedly, always keeping in mind the goal of understanding them without reference to notes. It is a great thrill to listen to a passage in a new language and to realize that you can understand the message directly without translating it into your own language and without even thinking about the grammatical structure that carries the message.

Under some circumstances you can get useful recordings of natural conversations and treat them as you have treated other recordings—getting a consultant to explain difficult parts and then listening until the message becomes transparent. If they can be understood, recordings of natural conversations are the best of all, but at about the time they become easy to use, you are likely to be able to leave such lessons behind.

The time will come when you can understand the natural conversations that surround you easily enough to make them the most useful means for further learning. Of course you will often miss things, but you will reach the point where your misunderstandings are sufficiently infrequent to allow you to stop people and ask them to explain on the spot. This will be a point of great emancipation. With the help of reasonably naturalistic recordings, you should be able to push your receptive ability to the point where you have a very good sense of the language and an excellent base upon which to build productive abilities as well.

An Interlude on Pronunciation

Up to now I have said little about pronunciation because it poses relatively few problems for the hearer, and, if a native-like pronunciation does not become a point of pride, it does not usually pose too many serious problems for a speaker either. Your new language may be filled with strange sounds, and you may not be able to figure out how people manipulate their tongues to produce these sounds, but as long as they do not speak too quickly and as long as they restrict their vocabulary, you should be able to hear well enough to know what words they are using. A modest amount of phonetic training may help you to pronounce things a bit better than you otherwise would. It may even help you to discriminate the sounds that you hear, but even without phonetic training you should be able to manage.

One of the sillier goals of recent language pedagogy, in fact, has been to push students to achieve a flawless accent. The goal is unobtainable for 99 percent of adults and unnecessary for anyone except those few who intend to become spies. Too much emphasis on pronunciation does little except foster discouragement and take up time that could be better spent on more important matters. No one really understands why some people acquire relatively "good" accents while others do not, but the fact is that some people do learn to speak understandably, and even fluently, while still retaining powerful foreign accents. The goal of a flawless accent, like the goal of being "adopted into the tribe," has more to do with vanity than with reality. I don't mean that you shouldn't do your best to pronounce things well, but you are not likely to hide the fact that you are a foreigner. That is a status you will have to accept. I will limit my phonetic advice to the lame suggestion that you should do your best to mimic what you hear.

There is, however, one principle of *phonology* (which is the study of the organization of speech sounds) in contrast to *phonetics* (which is the study of the sounds themselves) that you should understand clearly, for it really can help you with both comprehension and speaking. This is the principle of *contrast*. If you have ever had a course in linguistics, you should have learned all you need to know about contrast. In case you have not, I review the principle here.

The sounds of a language can be regarded as falling into a relatively small number of distinct or "contrasting" sets of sounds that we can call *phonemes*. You can think of the phonemes of a language as the sets of sounds that would be represented by distinct letters in a perfect spelling system. Thus in English we have a phoneme /k/ in such words as *keep, cool, scoop,* and *sack* and we ordinarily think that all these sounds are the "same." If you listen carefully, however, you will discover that they are by no means identical since the pronunciation of each /k/ is influenced by the sounds next to it. (English, having a much less than perfect spelling system, sometimes spells this phoneme with *k* and at other times with *c* or *ck,* but it is the sounds rather than the spellings that are relevant to this discussion.) However similar or different these various kinds of /k/'s are from one another, they are certainly more like one another than they are like /p/ or /t/ or /g/. (We write phonemes between slanting brackets. Whenever you see slants, you will know that it is pronunciation that is being referred to rather than spelling.) In English we say that /k/ contrasts with /p/ and /t/ and /g/ and with all the other phonemes of English. It is because these phonemes contrast with each other that it is possible to use them to keep words distinct. The differences between /k/, /p/, /t/, and /g/ are enough to keep *cot, pot, tot,* and *got* distinct. The different kinds of /k/ are not sufficiently different, in English, to distinguish different words.

This much seems obvious. The difficulties come when you find that other speakers, either those who speak different dialects of your own language or those who speak an entirely different language, make different contrasts than you do yourself. Within a single language most speakers make most of the same contrasts, but a few differences are found even there. Some speakers of English, but not all, make a contrast between the initial sounds of such pairs of words as *where/wear, whether/weather, why/Y, which/witch*, etc. If you find this hard to believe, inquire among your friends, and you are likely to find some people who make the contrast (and who thus pronounce the words of each pair differently) and others who do not (and for whom, therefore, these pairs of words are homophones).

The difficulties are compounded when we come to other languages, for here the contrasts may be very different from our own. In Chinese, otherwise identical syllables can contrast with each other in the relative pitch or "tone" with which they are pronounced. A syllable with a high tone such as /shī/ 'teacher' contrasts with one with rising tone such as /shí/ 'ten' or with a syllable that starts low, falls slightly, and then rises a bit again such as /shǐ/ 'arrow', and all three of these words contrast with a syllable that starts high and falls sharply such as /shì/ 'scholar'. Even though the consonants and vowels of these syllables are identical, the syllables contrast with one another because of their tones. They are, in fact, entirely different words. A student of Chinese needs to learn to discriminate these tonal contrasts in order to understand what others say and needs to be able to make them in order to be understood.

In many languages of India, some consonants are pronounced with a sharp puff of breath while others are pronounced without it, and these different consonants contrast sufficiently to keep words distinct. French has vowels that contrast with one another primarily in nasalization. No two languages have exactly the same system of contrasts. A few new contrasts will have to be learned with any new language.

Before you work on a language, you cannot know what contrasts it will have, and when you first start to listen you should probably not worry too much about the details. As you move along, however, you will want to gain a very solid grasp of your new language's system of contrasts. You must ask yourself which sounds contrast with which other sounds. Almost surely there will be some sounds that your consultants will insist are different, but which you will have some trouble hearing as different. In all probability, these will contrast in their language but not in yours.

When in doubt, you should look for so-called minimal pairs. These are pairs of words that are exactly alike in pronunciation except for one crucial contrast. *Pat* and *bat* are English minimal pairs for the /p/-/b/ contrast, while *pick* and *peek* differ only in their contrasting vowels. Spanish speakers have difficulty with this last pair, because Spanish lacks a contrast between these quite similar vowels. For some English speakers, but not for others, *which* and *witch* form a minimally contrasting pair. *Which* and *witch* are a good test pair to use if you want to find out whether a particular speaker makes this contrast. Look for similar test pairs in the language you are learning, and use the pairs to figure out what the contrasting sounds (phonemes) of your new language are.

Understanding the system of contrasts of your new language will allow you to focus upon what is important in its sound system and to ignore much of what is not crucial. Minor differences within phonemes (such as the differences among the various kinds of /k/'s in *keep, cool, walk*, etc.)

are much less important than the differences between contrasting phonemes. Only if you understand the system of contrasts can you ask sensible questions about the pronunciation that the speakers of your new language will readily understand. A question such as "Do you pronounce it *creek* or *crick*?" makes sense only on the assumption that the vowels in these two alternative pronunciations of the word do contrast. Understanding the system of contrasts will help you to categorize the sounds of a new word quickly and efficiently. By figuring out which phonemes are used in the word you will know how to pronounce it.

Anthropologists have an additional and more specific reason for working toward an understanding of the system of phonemic contrasts: the need to transcribe the language consistently. All anthropologists need to write down words from the language and many will want to transcribe longer passages, such as rituals or folklore. When a language has no conventional written form the only reasonable way to do transcription is to assign a letter to each phoneme and to write "phonemically." For a useful transcription, you should have different ways of writing every contrasting sound of the language—a letter, a letter with an accent, or, when necessary, a pair of letters—but you should avoid using different symbols for sounds that do not contrast. Thus, a phonemic analysis is necessary for recording anthropological information as well as for learning the language. Transcribing will become easier as you work toward writing each phoneme consistently with the same letter.

Most of the contrasts of the language will not cause you any great difficulty. They will be similar enough to the contrasts of your own language to seem quite natural. But there are likely to be a few troublesome contrasts and you should spend a little time making sure that you can at least hear the difference between the contrasting pairs. Among those that often cause trouble for English speakers, because they are not found in their language, are contrasts between long and short vowels, between aspirated and unaspirated consonants, and between tones, but there is no way to anticipate every possible problem. Find minimal pairs, and have a consultant pronounce them at random until you can tell, with some confidence, which he is saying. A modest amount of this kind of drill will improve your hearing and it will provide a good foundation for talking as well. Even if you have no illusions about passing yourself off as a native, you really ought to do your best to make all the contrasts that they make.

If you have a good understanding of the system of contrasts in the language, you will be able to write words that you hear in a consistent way, and you will know what you are aiming for when you try to use the word yourself. When you discover a contrast that is different from those in your own language, such as the contrast among different tones or the contrast between long and short vowels, it is better, when you begin to speak, to exaggerate the difference than to minimize it. Say the long vowels very long, and make the short vowels very, very short. Pronounce tones with exaggerated rises and falls—or with what seem like exaggerated rises and falls to you. If you go too far, it will be easy to moderate the difference later. If, on the other hand, you do not make the contrast sharp enough, you may be difficult to understand. You may even forget about the importance of the contrast and forget about exactly what you are aiming for.

In addition to the vowels and consonants, the sound system also includes intonation, stress, and rhythm, the ways in which we modulate our voices in pitch, volume, and timing. Vowels and consonants are represented in our writing system and perhaps this makes them seem relatively concrete and real. Intonation, on the other hand, is poorly represented in our writing, and we know less about how to analyze it. If your language has contrasting tones, you will have to work out a system of recording them, such as numbers next to the syllables or accents over the vowels, but recording or even analyzing the patterns of intonation that extend over whole phrases and sentences is even more difficult. Perhaps you can help yourself remember the intonation patterns if you put accents on syllables with heavy stress and decorate sentences with wavy lines that reflect the ups and downs of pitch. In the end, however, the only way you can you learn intonation is by listening carefully and by doing your best to imitate well.

It is worth remembering that intonation is learned very early in childhood. Even before children use words, they regularly produce intonation that reflects the language around them. American children babble in ways that sound like English. Japanese children babble in ways that sound like Japanese. But what is learned so early by children is often learned very imperfectly later. Intonation can be terribly elusive for the adult learner. The only advice I can offer about intonation is to tell you to listen. Listen and keep listening. Try to get a feeling for the way people use their voices. Before you can acquire reasonable intonation, you have to hear a great deal of the language. When you have heard enough, you should gain some sort of feeling for the intonational patterns, and you should then be able to mimic them to some extent.

Learning to draw is very largely a matter of learning how to look—to use your eyes. Learning to speak is very largely a matter of learning how to hear—to use your ears. Try to gain an understanding of what the distinctive sounds of the language are. That will help you to hear the language well. But when you start to speak, just about all you can do is mimic. Listen to yourself as you talk and ask yourself whether you are doing a plausible imitation of the people you have been listening to. You will not be perfect, but there are many degrees of imperfection. Your minimum goal, of course, will be for the people to understand what you are saying, and they ought to be able to understand easily, without having to strain. Beyond that, it is largely a question of aesthetics—or pride.

Another Interlude: Grammar

As I emphasize repeatedly in these pages, I think it is a great mistake to squander too much time or energy on the details of grammar. So concerned am I that you not become distracted by grammatical detail that I hestitate even to offer grammatical generalizations for fear that they will come to assume undue importance. Getting control of the vocabulary is really more essential and it should occupy more of your energies.

Nevertheless, a survey of a few of the broadest and most general grammatical patterns that you may face in your new language may help you to get a few things in focus relatively quickly and easily. In this section, I review some features of grammar that are widespread in the world's languages. If even this is too much grammar for your taste, I would encourage you to skip this section, but some learners may find it a help. Some of the broadest aspects of grammar can be considered under three headings: noun phrases, sentence patterns, and verb phrases. I will have a bit to say about each of these, and will finish with a few comments on ways of building up complex sentences.

Noun Phrases

All languages have names for things. In most languages these names fall into a grammatical class that deserves a distinctive label. Another way to say this is that words that translate *man, bird, star,* and *water* are all likely to be treated alike in the grammar. We may as well call these words by the familiar term *noun.* In all languages, moreover, nouns can come embedded in phrases in which they are surrounded by various modifying words, and everywhere we find modifiers of the following types: (1) demonstratives (*this, that,* etc.); (2) possessives, including possessive pronouns (*my, his, Mary's,* etc.); (3) numbers and other words of quantity (*five, many, some,* etc.); (4) adjectives, or words that translate our adjectives (*red, big, awful, unbelievable,* etc.); and (5) relative clauses (*who came in, that was lying on the table,* etc.). In addition, many languages, but by no means all, have articles (*a, the,* etc.). Languages that lack articles usually make heavy use of demonstratives where we might use a definite article (i.e., in the absence of *the* they may use *this* or *that*), and they tend to use the numeral *one* where we might use the indefinite article *a.*

In English, all of these constituents of the noun phrase, except for relative clauses, come before the noun. Thus we can say *my three big books that are on the table,* in which a possessive pronoun, a number, and an adjective occur before the noun (*books*) while a relative clause (*that are on the table*) occurs afterward. Together, these form a noun phrase. All languages seem to allow very similar noun phrase constituents, but the order in which the constituents occur differs from language to language. All the constituents may occur before the noun, or all may occur after the noun, or some may occur in front and others after. Like English, however, each individual language usually has a reasonably fixed order of constituents.

All languages seem to have three special classes of words—question words, pronouns, and proper names—that act in sentences rather like ordinary nouns, except that they rarely take modifiers. Modification may not be impossible with these words (*another what?*, *little me*, *big Bob*), but it is hardly typical. Ordinary nouns are frequently joined by one or more modifying words.

In some languages some constituents of the noun phrase must "agree," in one way or another, with the noun. In a number of European languages, for instance, adjectives and articles must agree with the noun in gender, number, or case. Thus, when a French adjective is used to modify a noun that is feminine and plural, the adjective must also be put in a feminine and plural form. Nouns in the Bantu languages of Africa fall into several different classes and other elements of the noun phrase must reflect the class of the noun with which they are used. The same prefix may then need to be attached to several successive members of the noun phrase. Agreement of this sort can be a considerable annoyance to early speakers of a language who feel that they must get everything exactly right, since the correct form of modifiers can only be chosen after remembering the class of the noun. From the point of view of the listener, on the other hand, agreement can be of some assistance, since it may help to sort out which words are most closely related to one another as parts of the same noun phrase.

You may make more rapid progress if you keep your ears open for the expectable constituents of noun phrases and if you take note of the order in which they conventionally occur in your language. You will understand more quickly, and eventually make yourself more understandable, if you can get the constituents of your noun phrases in the right order. Noun phrases are usually simple enough so that this should not be difficult to do.

Sentence Patterns

A very common sentence pattern in all languages is formed from a verb and one or more associated noun phrases: *The man admires the girl, Ralph gave the bullwhip to a child, I will see her in the afternoon.* In these examples *the man, the girl, Ralph, the bullwhip, to a child, I,* and *in the afternoon* are noun phrases, while *admires, gave,* and *will see* are the verbs. Just as we can consider noun phrases to be formed around a central noun, so we can consider many sentences to be formed around a central verb.

The noun phrases in these sentences fill roles that have been identified by a confusing range of terms, but we may as well use the familiar *subject* (e.g., *Ralph*), *direct object* (e.g., *the bullwhip*), and *indirect object* (e.g., *a child*). A number of other types of noun phrases can be added to these three, the most important of which are phrases that locate the action in time and space. These usually require prepositions in English and so are often called *prepositional phrases,* but they can also be called *locatives* (e.g., *in the afternoon, on the table,* etc.).

Every language has the problem of making clear how

each noun phrase is related to its verb. The hearer has to be able to tell which noun phrase is the subject, which is the object, etc. In many cases the plausible semantic relationship among the constituents makes this fairly easy. In *Bob chopped down the tree* it is unlikely that it was the tree that did the chopping. When you first try to understand a language, the plausible semantic relationships offer the most accessible clues to the organization of the parts of a sentence. In *Mary saw Bill,* however, Mary and Bill are both capable of either seeing or being seen, so plausible semantic relationships are not enough. In English, of course, the word order shows very clearly which noun phrase has which function, for the subject comes in front of the verb while most other noun phrases follow. In *John gave me his sister,* we also rely on word order to show that *me* is the indirect object and *sister* the direct.

If we say, instead, *John gave his sister to me* we have added a word, *to,* that makes clear that *me* is still the indirect object in spite of its changed location in the sentence. This is an example of a third means (in addition to word order and reliance upon plausible semantic relationships) of keeping the noun phrases sorted out: the addition of extra words or affixes to the noun phrases. All languages have markers that, under some circumstances, attach to nouns or to noun phrases and that show how the nouns are related to the verb and to the rest of the sentence. In English, our markers go before the rest of the noun phrase and we call them *prepositions.* In many languages they come after the noun or after the entire noun phrase, and then they are known as *postpositions.* Case markers that show whether a noun is nominative (subject), accusative (object), or locative, etc., are similar to postpositions except that they have been fused more tightly to their noun. One important use of pre- and postpositions is with noun phrases that indicate position or direction of movement in time or in space (*at home, from the beach, on Tuesday, until then,* etc.), but they are also used to show many other relationships (*with, by means of, for, on behalf of, instead of,* etc.).

In many languages, as in English, the most common order of major sentence constituents is Subject-Verb-Object (SVO), but in some languages the verb comes either first or last in the sentence instead. In verb-first and verb-last languages there is often a degree of flexibility in the relative order of the noun phrases, and marking by prepositions, postpositions, or case markers then becomes more crucial than in a language where word order is more rigid. Nevertheless, when the verb comes first or last the most common major constituent orders are VSO and SOV. Languages in which the usual word order is VOS, OVS, or OSV are unusual, but these orders may occur occasionally as a way of emphasizing one of the constituents.

A fourth way of showing the relationship of the noun phrases to the verb is by marking the verb. We do this in English with passive sentences. *The dog was bitten by John* clearly means something different than *The dog bit John* even though, in both sentences, *dog* precedes the verb and *John* follows it. In this example the reversed meaning of the noun phrases in the passive sentence is shown, in part, by the preposition *by* that goes with *John,* but it is also shown by the *was* and *-en* that mark the verb.

You may find it helpful to pay a bit of attention to the order of the major constituents of sentences and to locate the means by which the noun phrases are related to the verb.

Most languages have one or more classes of words that we can call, a bit loosely, *adverbs,* and that carry such meanings as *quickly, happily, fortunately, tomorrow, now.* The details that govern the use of such words can be quite messy. Sometimes they act rather like nouns, sometimes like verbs, and sometimes only like themselves. It may be useful to look upon some of them, along with the noun phrases, as constituents of the sentence, but particles with adverbial-like meanings may also come attached to other words as affixes. All you can do is keep a look out for places where adverbial-like meanings are introduced into a sentence and imitate what you hear.

Most sentences in most languages have at least one verb, but a somewhat less important sentence type can sometimes be found, the *equational* sentence, in which two noun phrases are equated to one another. In standard English we must relate the two noun phrases by means of a form of *be: I am a man, That kid is a looser, Apples are fruit.* In some languages, including some nonstandard dialects of English, the noun phrases are simply placed side by side without any supporting verb: *I a man, Tomatoes really fruit too.*

Verb Phrases

The verb can be regarded as the central element of most sentences, the keystone that holds together the various adverbs, question words, pronouns, and noun phrases. In addition, and more centrally, the verb may also be the focus of a number of more closely related items that make up a verb phrase. The constituents of verb phrases are considerably more variable from language to language than are the constituents of noun phrases, so it is more difficult to give reliable guidance about what you are likely to find. Verbs, in fact, are a point of great linguistic variability, and all I can do is suggest some likely constituents and leave you to explore.

Markers of tense and aspect are, perhaps, the most common additional elements of a verb phrase. Tenses locate the action of the verb and of the sentence in time. We often think of the significant tenses as *past, present,* and *future,* but languages vary greatly in the divisions of time that are distinguished by the tenses. Tense can be shown by separate words that are used with the verb (*did walk/will walk*), by affixes that are joined to the verb (*walk/walked*), or by some kind of change of the verb itself (*see/saw; go/went*). Aspect is not an obligatory grammatical category of English, so it is more difficult to give simple examples that seem clear to English speakers, but many languages require verbs to be marked in a way that shows, for instance, whether the action takes place at a single moment, repeatedly, over a long period of time, etc. In English we can express such ideas, when we need them, with adverbs such as *regularly, now and then, continuously, just then,* etc., but in some languages markers of aspect are required with every verb.

One constituent of the English verb phrase is the class of *modal* verbs: *would, should, can, may, must,* etc. All languages need to have some way of indicating such concepts as necessity, obligation, permission, ability, and likelihood. These are often expressed by means of auxiliary verbs that are used in association with the main verb of the sentence, but details vary from one language to another. All languages also need to indicate negation. The most common negation sign is, typically, associated with the verb—sometimes as an affix attached to the verb, sometimes as a separate word that is placed in the vicinity of the verb.

In many languages, verbs must be decorated with affixes that show something about the subject or the object or the indirect object. These affixes can be thought of as similar to pronouns except that they attach to the verb. English has a hint of this pattern in its third person singular *-s* that must be added to the verb under some circumstances, and some familiar European languages have a considerably wider range of person markers that agree with the subject in both person and number. Far more complex systems are found in some non-European languages where verbs must be marked not only to reflect the subject, but also one or more objects. It is as if a sentence with three noun phrases had to have all three reflected in the verb, something like this: *John he-her-it-gave the book to Mary.*

A few languages require every verb or sentence to be marked with some indication of how the speaker knows what he is saying, whether through direct observation, through hearsay, or because it is general knowledge, etc. Some languages distinguish between causative and noncausative verbs, requiring a different form of the verb in *John caused-to-close the door* than in *the door closed.* It is quite impossible to list every possibility that you may run into. All you can do is keep your ears open.

One final point may be worth mentioning. Many languages have two or three very common verbs that fill a variety of central grammatical functions. The English verbs *have* and *be* are of this sort. Notice that each of these verbs has a number of different uses. *Have* can show various sorts of possession while *be* is used to show several quite diverse meanings: location (*John is in Chicago*), equality (*John is the man you saw*), class membership (*John is a human being*), predicate adjective (*John is miserable*), and as an auxiliary verb associated with the suffix *-ing* (*John is walking*). Different languages group these meanings in quite different ways. Some languages have different verbs for *inalienable* possession (*He has-permanently a nose, He has-permanently a mother*) and *alienable* possession (*He has-temporarily a shirt*). Some languages use the same verb for both possession and location (*He is-at Port Moresby, Only one eye is-at Raoul* 'Raoul has only one eye'). Some languages require separate verbs for location, equality, and class membership. In some languages meanings that we convey by means of adjectives are conveyed instead by words that act like verbs, so that sentences with a form something like *John glads* or *Mary beautifuls* are used instead of *John is glad* or *Mary is beautiful*. You have to adapt yourself to the particular patterns you face and not expect to find close parallels to English. Nevertheless, all languages need to have ways of expressing all these meanings, and the differences lie in how different meanings are grouped, not in what meanings are expressible.

The verb and the verb phrase may be as complicated as any part of your new language. If this is the case you cannot expect to master them all at once. You will, however, be able to understand and even to get your meaning across without all the fine details.

Combining Sentences
One point of great linguistic complexity lies in the way that simple sentences can be combined into more complex ones. Or, perhaps it is more accurate to say that linguists have described some complex sentences as if they are formed from

combinations of two or more simpler sentences, and this leads to very complex linguistic descriptions. At the most extreme, linguists may describe every single verb as deriving from an originally independent sentence. For a practical language learner a somewhat less involuted attitude usually suffices. You need to worry about meaning, and it may not always be very useful to think of the parts of a sentence as having derived from something else, but there are times when this viewpoint can help to make the organization of complex sentences seem reasonable.

The easiest way of building up complex sentences is by means of simple coordinating conjunctions, and here it is straightforward to regard the constituents as deriving from separate sentences. Most languages have some sort of equivalents to English *and, but,* and *or* that can be used to string sentences together. Some people join most of their successive sentences together with particles that mean little more than *and then, and so, and having done that,* etc., the main purpose of which seems to be to show that all that is said is part of the same discourse.

Sometimes more essential meaning is carried by the words that join sentences. You may find phrases that correspond more or less to *before, because of, otherwise, if that is not the case,* and that are used to show relationships among clauses (as sentences are called once they are joined together as constituents of a larger sentence): *She took a shower before she climbed into bed. Because it was snowing, he decided not to walk.* Linguistic descriptions of such phenomena can grow exceedingly complex because sentences must often be modified when they are joined together as clauses—some parts added and others left out. In addition to *She took a shower before she climbed into bed* we can also say *She took a shower before climbing into bed,* where we omit the second *she* and change the form of the verb from *climbed* to *climbing.* For the practical language learner, highly abstract rules that precisely describe changes of this sort are usually more bother than they are worth. When you are listening you must first understand the major words so that you know what the subject matter is, and the general context will then often be sufficient to tell you about the relationship among the various things referred to. What is most crucial in the beginning is enough flexibility to accept whatever you hear, and enough imagination to recognize the relationships among the words. An early speaker can usually express these relationships in a simpler way without needing the more elaborate constructions.

Some languages are far freer than English in stringing several verbs together. People may say things such as *I will go-walk-find the basket* or *He entered-sat-talked.* Special affixes may (or may not) show the relationships among such verbs but, again, you will need to worry more about the meaning conveyed by joined verbs than about the syntactic rules by which they are joined.

In most languages some verbs call for other verbs. English verbs such as *need, wonder, believe, want, demand, like,* and many others, are often used with clauses that contain other verbs: *I need to go, I wonder if he will come, I wonder what he is doing, I believe that they are swimming, I want to find out, I demand that you stop that at once, I like throwing rocks.* The variety of constructions of this sort may be quite wide. Indeed, these few examples from English hint at a considerable range of constructions, some requiring infinitive verbs (with *to*), others allowing verbs with *-ing,* and still others requiring clauses that are introduced by *if, what,* or *that.*

Once again, the practical language learner needs to worry much more about the meaning of such sentences than about their syntactic details. If you are confident that a word that you hear means *wonder* or *believe* or *demand,* your most essential need will be to know what the other words around it mean. If you understand the meanings of the major words, the meaningful relationships among them will probably be clear even if the syntactic details are not. It is more difficult to reproduce all these patterns correctly, but the best foundation for doing so is intimate familiarity with them through understanding.

Relative clauses form one other important means of building up the complexity of a sentence and they can be looked upon as deriving from independent sentences. For instance, *who stole all the fine porcelain* is a relative clause and it can occur as part of a noun phrase such as *the misguided felon who stole all the fine porcelain.* A relative clause can be reasonably regarded as having been derived from an independent sentence, in this case *The misguided felon stole all the fine porcelain.* One simply replaces *The misguided felon* with *who* and the result is a relative clause that can be used to modify a noun. Since relative clauses tend to show many characteristics of sentences (they include a verb and they may come with auxiliaries, objects, locatives, adverbs, etc., as well), you may find it helpful to think of relative clauses as being derived from sentences. Once again, however, it is the meaningful relationships among the parts that should interest you most, and these relationships will emerge most clearly when you understand the meanings of the individual words.

There is no knowing ahead of time which grammatical patterns will be found in your language or to know which will cause you the most problems. The comments in this section are intended to do no more than give you some idea of the range of central grammatical patterns that crop up in languages, and perhaps they will help you to close in on what is most essential but, for the most part, you will be on your own. You have to expect to spend many long months before you can understand all the details, and years may be required before you can reproduce them all perfectly. You will be able to communicate successfully long before every detail is mastered.

3 Moving Ahead: Production

Talking

During your early months in the field I have encouraged you to focus most of your deliberate study on comprehension, and in the previous chapter I offered a number of suggestions about how to work as rapidly as possible toward an ability to understand the language. Unless you are working among a group (such as many North American Indians) where English is so well known that you find it difficult to say anything at all at first, I expect that you will both need and want to start talking very soon, but I have encouraged you to let talking come as a by-product of learning to understand. Only *after* you have learned enough so that, when people make a reasonable effort, they can make themselves understood to you quite easily, will it finally become worthwhile to make a more concerted effort to learn to speak. At this point, speaking will come most easily if you think of yourself as converting what you already know (i.e., what you can already understand) to productive use. The next sections offer suggestions about how to speed up your ability to speak, but I want you to think of them as techniques that allow you to build upon what you have already learned to understand.

I have argued that the most important thing you need for understanding is vocabulary, and I have encouraged you to spend most of your energy building up your comprehension vocabulary. I would urge a parallel strategy for production. If you are willing to plunge ahead without worrying about grammatical niceties, you will find that you can express almost any meaning with words. The kinds of meaning that are conveyed in languages by grammatical categories such as tense or plurality, and by grammatical processes such as prefixation, suffixation, or internal change, can almost always be expressed in alternative ways by means of words. In English, for instance, we have a tense system that conveys something about time relationships, but it is also possible to convey these time relationships by means of adverbs such as *tomorrow, this morning, later, four o'clock,* and so forth. Similarly, the meaning carried by the English plural can be conveyed, instead, by numbers or by words such as *many* or *lots of.* Demonstratives (*this, that,* etc.) can do the work of the definite article (*the*). *One* can do the work of *a.* Instead of the comparative suffix *-er* in *slower* we can use a separate word, *more slow,* and we would even understand *more big.* Languages with grammatical aspect also have separate words, often adverbs, that express similar concepts. Languages with person affixes on verbs also have independent pronouns, but if even the pronouns are too difficult one can always resort to the noun or personal name for which the pronoun would stand. Since it is usually considerably easier to use independent words than grammatical processes, you can, in the beginning, say much of what you want to say with words.

Usually the only grammatical patterns that deserve any appreciable self-conscious attention, in the earliest stages of talking, are those of word order. You will certainly make yourself understood much more easily if you get your words in a reasonably conventional order. Notice the order of the major elements in the sentence. Does the verb come first, last, or in the middle? Do they say *Hits Bill the man, Bill the man hits,* or *Bill hits the man?* Where do demonstratives (*this, that,* etc.) and numbers go with respect to nouns and adjectives? As soon as you start to string two or three words together, you should do your best to get them in the right order.

If affixes carry important meaning, you may also need to reach for a few of them quite early. But to the extent that affixes are crucial, they are also likely to be both quite salient and quite stable, indeed quite like a word, and thus easy to recognize and to reproduce. To the extent that affixes are complex and irregular, they are also likely to be relatively unimportant. You may sound funny if you leave them out or use the wrong one, but that is not likely to make you particularly difficult to understand. Focusing your efforts on words and refusing to become overly concerned with grammatical subtleties will undeniably leave you speaking an imperfect, even broken form of your new language, but nothing can really save you from that. I would even suggest that by accepting early broken speech you will be acquiring language in the most natural possible way. Broken speech has another important function—it signals to the listener that the speaker is not fluent, and it invites careful speech in return. Some early learners are far too fluent for their own good, for they elicit floods of free but totally incomprehensible language. Since such learners cannot answer back, the conversation comes to a crashing halt and the chance for useful practice is lost.

When children first learn to speak, they go through a period of baby talk and garbled grammar. When uneducated adults of varied language background are thrown together in a situation where they simply have to communicate, they devise pidgin languages of minimal complexity to achieve their pragmatic ends. The ingenious tourist uses his twenty words of Greek to supplement his gestures and to get his needs across. These people accomplish their goals with little concern for linguistic niceties. Scholars, however, have higher goals, and they may worry so much about making mistakes that they become afraid to open their mouths. I want to persuade you that the shortest route to speaking a language is to blunder ahead in situations where you want to get some sort of meaning across and where you are not overly concerned with correctness. You can fake most pronunciation and a great deal of grammar, and I think you should be content with anything that will make yourself understood. You cannot possibly fake vocabulary, however, and when you start to speak, it will be vocabulary, above all, for which you will have to grope. If you can get out enough words, you will be able to make your meaning known, even if you string your words together in a strange order and pronounce them with only a loose approximation to native standards. But however you pronounce them and however you string them together, you will need words.

As an example of how you can convey your meaning with minimal grammar, consider the following passage, written first in conventional English, and then in a sort of mangled but still understandable pidgin.

"Where are you going?"
"I'm going to the market to look for a piece of cloth for a skirt."

"Are there likely to be a lot of people selling cloth there now?"

"Oh yes, today is market day, so all the cloth sellers have come to sell their goods."

"You go where?"

"To market. Me want cloth. Make skirt."

"At market maybe many people sell cloth today, huh?"

"Yes, yes. Market day today. All cloth people come sell cloth."

This is hardly an elegant way to speak, and it surely misses some of the subtler points of the grammatically correct version, but it does convey the major ideas in an understandable way. To talk this way is to exploit your available resources for practical purposes without getting hung up on details. It amounts to a sort of personal pidgin language. A pidgin is the adult equivalent of the baby talk that all children pass through in learning their first language, and there is no more reason to fear that an adult's pidgin will become frozen than to suppose that children will never outgrow their baby talk. It does help to get the words in a more or less conventional order, but beyond that, little is crucial except pulling out enough words.

I do not think it is ever necessary to invent a pidgin deliberately. On the contrary, a pidgin is simply what emerges naturally when anyone presses an incipient ability to the limit. The strategies demonstrated by the passage about the cloth market are available to everyone. I emphasize the value of a pidgin not because I think you have to struggle to invent one, but because I expect that you will invent one quite naturally and you may need reassurance that this is a reasonable way to proceed. I think you should feel confident that you are speaking in a reasonable and useful way. Above all, instead of feeling embarrassed by your broken language, I think you should take great satisfaction in your cleverness at expressing yourself with such a rudimentary linguistic ability. A pidginized language of this sort is a practical intermediate goal for anyone in the field who wants to begin to talk. How do you get there?

If, at first, your speech comes primarily as a by-product of learning to understand, I suspect you will discover that you can start to use certain words much more easily than others. In particular, I expect that names for visible, concrete objects—animals, foods, common material objects—will be quite easy. Easiest of all, perhaps, will be names of objects not found in your own culture and for which the only name you know comes from your new language. In a sense, even names for places and people belong in this category. You will learn many proper names in your first month in the field, and while we do not usually reckon these as counting toward learning a foreign language, they are still words, and learning them is by no means a trivial task.

You may also find some common verbs and adjectives to be fairly easy, especially those that stand for relatively concrete or visible activities and qualities, such as *talk, eat, black,* and *big.* Pronouns and numbers may not be too bad. Prefixes and suffixes are likely to be more difficult. Abstract words are always difficult.

You will probably also find that searching your mind for words that you want to use is a very different process from searching your mind for the meaning of a word that you encounter. When you work to memorize a word in the foreign-to-meaning direction, you must start with its sounds (or spelling). The words that you are most likely to confuse in this case are those that sound (or look) somewhat alike. There is no particular likelihood that you will confuse words of similar meaning.

When you try to recall a word for active use in speaking, on the other hand, you will have to start with the meaning that you want to convey, and work from that meaning to a word that will express it. You will probably find that when you want the word for *dog,* you will search your mind for animal names and try to locate the right animal name for the domestic canine. If you want the word for *six* you will search among the numbers. This means that when working to improve *productive* vocabulary, it makes sense to categorize words according to their meaning, a categorization that is of little use for comprehension.

As you work to recall words for active use, you are likely to discover, to your dismay, that some words that you have learned to recognize and understand easily will be discouragingly difficult to retrieve. It would be nice to imagine that, once you have gained a sufficiently easy ability to understand a word, producing it would follow along with little effort. Perhaps it would come without effort if you had enough time to wait, but time is not what you are likely to have in unlimited quantity. Sooner or later a little systematic effort should help your production to progress more rapidly. The next three sections offer some suggestions that may help you when that time comes.

Vocabulary and Semantic Range

When learning to use words, you must always be sensitive to the varied ways in which different languages assign meaning. You should never expect to find words in your new language that correspond exactly to the familiar words of English. If, in the past, you have studied only European languages, you may be surprised at how different word meanings can be. Common historical origins and a long common cultural tradition have led to many parallelisms among the languages of Europe, so that it often happens that words in one language have reasonably exact translations in other languages. Even metaphors and proverbs come to be shared by languages that have been in long and intimate contact.

Even in a language as closely related to English as Swedish, however, we find meanings of unexpected range. Where in English we can use the single word *think,* Swedes must choose among three quite separate words. *Tänka* means *think* in the sense of ponder or cogitate: *I will think the matter over.* *Tro* means *believe* where belief rests upon verifiable fact of some sort, as in *I think the train is due at five o'clock.* *Tänka* would be quite impossible in this case. On the other hand, in a sentence such as *I think roses are beautiful flowers* still another verb is called for, *tycka.* Here the matter rests neither upon cogitation or upon verifiable fact, but upon personal preference, upon what is liked or disliked. The distinctions among these three words are strange to English speakers but they must be learned by anyone who wants to speak understandable Swedish.

When learning a language remote from the European tradition, you must expect the meaning of most words to differ, in some degree, from the meaning of familiar English words. Anthropologists will not be surprised when kinship terms are assigned in very different ways from English so that, for instance, mother's brother, father's brother, mother's sister's husband, and father's sister's husband may all be called by different terms. Different verbs may be required for *change clothes, change buses, change money, change one's mind,* and *change into a witch.*

Even such a straightforward term as *hand* may not have a simple translation. Some people have a single word that covers both *hand* and *arm,* while others have one word for the hand and lower arm and another word for the upper arm. Even if there is a word close in literal meaning to English *hand* you are unlikely to be able to use it in phrases equivalent to *please hand me the basket,* to say nothing of *on the other hand.* There are likely to be formal/polite and informal/rude alternatives for some concepts where we would be content with a single word. Repeatedly, you will find that where a single word suffices in English, a choice between two or more words will be needed in your new language. Reciprocally, of course, there will be areas of meaning where your new language will have a single word that covers the range of several English words.

An entire book could be devoted to describing the full meaning and use of a single word. To specify what it can refer to, what it cannot refer to, who can use it under what circumstances, to characterize its degree of formality and all its subtle connotations, and to indicate its precise syntactical limitations can be such a complex task as to frighten a new learner into feeling that it is dangerous to use a word before learning a great deal about it. But word meanings are not chaotic. They are coherent enough in their own terms even when different from anything you have encountered before. It is a fatal mistake to postpone using a word for fear that you do not know enough about it. You simply must act with imperfect knowledge. You have to experiment, to guess, to use a word that you hope will be right in the situation. When you guess right, you will gain courage to repeat the word the next time. When you guess wrong, people may laugh and tell you how you should have said it, or they may look puzzled and give you a chance to explain yourself. In either case you will have learned something.

By learning the range and limits of the meanings of words you will also learn a great deal about the culture. You will learn what is important enough to the speakers to deserve a rich vocabulary. You will learn what distinctions the people find important enough to take notice of. To some extent, by learning their words, you will be learning to see the world in their terms. And that is a considerable part of what an anthropologist's job is all about.

The Functional Vocabulary

Names for concrete objects and relatively concrete verbs and adjectives may come fairly easily, and the irregular details of grammar may not matter much at first, but in between these extremes are found a number of groups of function words for which you are likely to find yourself groping. A bit of deliberate attention to these function words is likely to be particularly helpful. I would not work very hard to elicit such words systematically from your consultants. The particular words required will differ from language to language, and if you rely too much on deliberate elicitation you may bias your results in the direction of your own expectations. As you begin to gain some ability to understand, however, you will often hear words cropping up in the speech of others that belong to these groups. You can then make note of them, just as you make note of all important words, and later you can learn to use them actively. I suggest, in particular, that words or phrases of the following semantic groups are likely to be useful. You may even come to need them in approximately the order that I list them.

Greetings and Courtesy Words

Among all people there are conventional ways of greeting others, of saying farewell, of showing courtesy. Not everyone has close equivalents of our own *hello, goodbye,* or *please,* and if your new language has no equivalent for *thank you,* you may have to struggle *against* an ingrained habit of mumbling "Thank you" when that would be appropriate in English. Still, all people have some frequently used expressions that accomplish similar tasks as our greetings and courtesy words. Instead of our conventional *How are you?,* some people use an equally conventional *Where are you going?* Some people have a courtesy word that they use when offering something to another person. Listen to others, note their courtesy words, and try to learn to use them.

Quantity

Your new language may or may not have some sort of grammatical plural, but even if it does, you will probably find it much easier, as well as much more precise, to convey a sense of quantity by words. In most places the numbers will be needed very early, but you will also want words for the ideas that we express by *many, only, a little, times* (as in *five times*), *first, second, several, most, both, too much, one more, approximately, whole, a lot, almost, enough.* You will want to know how people express measurements of length, volume, and weight.

Modals

The meanings that English conveys by means of its modal auxiliary verbs are of great help in modulating the sense you want to convey and even in showing a sense of courtesy. You will probably find that you want to convey such meanings as *can, will, would, should, must, must not, don't have to, need, could, may.*

Pronouns

You will very soon want words for *I, you, we, they*, etc. All people have pronouns, but don't be surprised if the pronouns you hear do not correspond exactly to those in your own language. Some people make no distinction between *he* and *she*. Some *do* make a distinction between two kinds of *we—you and I* versus *(s)he and I.* Some people have to select among pronouns according to whom they are speaking to and how polite they want to be. These distinctions may be far more complex than the relatively simple two-way distinction found in some European languages between polite and familiar equivalents for *you* (e.g., the French distinction between *vous* and *tu*). The pronouns of some languages have annoyingly many forms—such as our own subject and object pronouns (*I* versus *me*), but often there will be one form that is most easily understood and you can use it to make your meaning clear even if you can't, at first, master all the varied forms, as in the famous *Me Tarzan, her Jane.* If verbs take person affixes you will certainly want to work toward being able to use them, but they may not be crucial at first if you can use easier independent pronouns instead.

Questions and Answers

You will very quickly need question words such as *where, when, what, how many, who, how, how long, which, why, what time.* Some languages have handy question particles that can be tacked onto the beginning or end of a sentence to turn it into a question, and such a particle is wonderfully useful. You will also need ways of responding to questions: *yes, no, I don't know, right, of course.* Don't be dismayed, however, if your language doesn't have simple equivalents for all of these words. In some languages you can't just say "*No*" in answer to a question like "Did he come?" but you have to say something like "Not come." Listen to the way they answer questions and follow their lead. Questions are also an area where you should be particularly sensitive to appropriate cultural usage. Notice what kinds of questions can be asked on what occasions.

Coordinating Conjunctions

Keep your ears open for words corresponding to *and, but, if, not, or,* and *also.* Make note of them. You will want to use them.

Indefinites

As you begin to gain some modest ability to get your ideas across, you will probably find yourself groping for indefinite words with such meanings as *some, any, all, no, none, every, always, sometimes, never, everything, something, nothing, anything, everyone, someone, no one, anyone, everywhere, somewhere, nowhere, anywhere.*

Time Words

Typically, the expression of time is a highly complicated matter. Tense systems can be very difficult to master, but most of what you will really need in the early stages of your language learning can be expressed with words. There will probably be large numbers of such words, however, and some deliberate effort with them should pay off: *morning, evening, night, today, yesterday, tomorrow, this morning, tomorrow morning, tonight, last night, minute, hour, day, week, month, year* (or whatever their units of time are); *last year, next year,* etc.; *ago, from now on, before, after, while, earlier, later, last, soon, quickly, future, right away, time, what time?* Names for the days of the week and the months are very useful if the people use them. After a few weeks of working on the language it will probably be worthwhile to start making a list of the time words that you have heard so that when you are ready you will be able to learn to use them as well as to understand them.

Place

The expression of location and position is generally less difficult than the expression of time. In part, this is because you can point in order to indicate your meaning and, in part, because place names can be used relatively easily to express location. A few words such as *this, that, here, there, left, right,* and *straight ahead* are useful.

Prepositions/Postpositions

All languages have either prepositions or postpositions, and the differences between the two lies merely in whether they come before or after the noun or noun phrase that they accompany. The prepositions or postpositions show something about the relationship of their noun phrase to other parts of the sentence, and many pre- and postpositions indicate location or movement. Their use is often highly eccentric and the details may take a long time to master, but you will find at least a few of them essential. (You will confuse your listeners if you don't get them on the correct side of the noun. Imagine how confused you would be if someone said *I went town to Bill with* instead of *I went to town with Bill.*) You may be able to find pre- or postpositions that do some of the work of English *in, on, at, at the place of, by, between, to, from, through, with, without, for, of, beside, instead of, according to.* Some languages also have case markers that act very much like pre- or postpositions and that indicate whether the noun phrase to which they are attached is a subject, object, indirect object, etc. Learning to use these case markers is likely to clarify your sentences considerably and to make it much easier for people to understand you.

Aspect

Some languages have a grammatical category known as *aspect.* Aspect is not an obligatory category in English, but we do have words that accomplish some of the same things that aspect markers accomplish in other languages. Whether or not your new language has grammatical aspect, you will want to be able to express such meanings as *begin, end, still, no longer, again, now and then, not yet, continue.* You may find these expressions quite difficult to learn, but they provide an important way of modulating your meaning.

Verbs of Movement and Position

You will also want a considerable number of words (verbs in most languages) to show how people move around or stay put: *go, come, ride, drive, move, travel, dwell, sit, stand, lie, open, close, take, bring, get, carry, arrive, leave, enter.* Except for their numbers, these are likely to be somewhat easier to learn than aspect words. The particular meanings that will be most essential vary from one language to another, and you should not expect to find simple equivalents for our English words. Notice which words your friends use and follow their lead.

Cognitive and Sensory Verbs

As you begin to gain some fluency you will want another set of meanings that are conveyed in most languages by verbs, and that have to do with the way we understand things and the way we perceive: *know, believe, think, suppose, imagine, like, forget, remember, see, look at, appear, look for, find, lose, hear, listen to, sound, taste.*

Conjunctions

A few simple conjunctions, such as *and, or,* and *but* are needed very early, but later you will also need more precise ways of connecting different ideas and expressions: *then, therefore, however, in order to, so that, on account of, even if, in spite of, especially, before, after, while, still, already.* As always, the particular ways in which these ideas are expressed will vary from one language to another, but you can be confident that your language will express them somehow.

Probability and Attitude

As your language improves, you will want to let people know how you feel about things, and you will want to give an indication of how likely you think things are to happen. You can accomplish your purposes with words that have such meanings as *of course, maybe, really, possibly, usually, hardly, unfortunately, luckily, importantly, hopefully, horribly.*

The categories given so far will not give you specific vocabulary for particular topics, but will provide, instead, a verbal matrix that forms the context for talking about all sorts of other more concrete topics. You will need them whatever your conversation is about. In addition, there are two substantive topics that usually arise repeatedly when one first reaches the field, language and shopping. Some early attention to them will be useful. Beyond these, you will need a great number of other content words.

Words about Language

When you first start to speak a language, language itself is such an intensely salient topic that you will immediately find yourself wanting to talk about it. You will find it useful to have the local equivalents for such words as *talk, ask* (a question), *answer, understand, be called, language, word, mean, meaning, translate,* etc.; and, if the people are literate, you will also want such words as *read, write, letter,* etc. It will also be useful to know the names of the various languages that your people know about. A few simple sentences, such as *What did you say?, What is the name for this?,* and *Can you speak more slowly?* will make your life much easier.

Money and Shopping

Unless you are in one of the few remote spots in the world where commerce has not yet penetrated, you will need words for money and shopping. You will want to know the names of coins and units of currency, as well as how to express amounts of money in ways that people readily understand. You will also want words such as *buy, sell, pay, cost,* and a general term for *money.*

Content Words

Individually, the *content* words are likely to be a good deal easier to learn than the more supportive and contextualizing functional vocabulary that was listed in the previous section. Words for relatively concrete or visible objects, actions, and qualities are, for some reason, far easier to fix in memory. The difficulties with the content words lie in their huge numbers. Every language has many thousands of content words, so they offer plenty of challenge. Each language, and even each situation, calls for its own vocabulary, so there is no way to give an exact list of words that you will need, but it may be useful to have a checklist of some likely areas of vocabulary for which to be on the lookout. Among other things, you will probably want words for most or all of the following.

Natural phenomena of the earth, sky, and water, including the weather (*stone, lake, mountain, rain,* etc.)

Animals, both domestic and wild, including various types of insects, and species of birds and fish

Plants, both wild and cultivated, from grasses and mushrooms to trees, as well as plant parts and plant products

Foods, drinks, and their preparation, including both ingredients and completed dishes

Body parts, internal as well as visible, of animals as well as of humans

People of various ages, sexes, and social categories (*man, woman, youth,* etc.)

Kinship terms

Work and occupations

Clothing and bodily adornment, cloth and other materials, sewing equipment and sewing techniques

Artifacts of the culture—baskets, traps, tools—and the materials and techniques for producing them

Buildings, building materials, parts of buildings, spatial arrangements, uses of buildings

Furniture, bedding, living patterns

Community and territorial divisions and organization

Government offices, departments, functions

Markets, shops, economy

Measures of distance, area, volume, value, time, etc.

Transportation, communication, carrying, traveling, vehicles

Socialization and education

Games and entertainment

Religion, festivals, gods, spirits, ceremonies

Birth, life cycle, and death

Illness, medicines, curing

Touch, taste, smell, sound (noises of various types, pitch, volume, etc.), sight (shape, color, etc.)

Human qualities—character, temperament, manner, behavior

Sentiments, thoughts, emotions

As you think about these categories, the words that occur to you first may be nouns—the names of things—but
most of the categories also include verbs. English, like
most other languages, has verbs associated with weather,
agriculture, cooking, movements and uses of the body, in-
terpersonal relations, work, dress, manufacture of goods of
all sorts, and with our economic, political, and educational
life. This means that these are not simply categories of
names of objects, but of cultural areas that include actions
and qualities as well.

As a list such as this is expanded, it begins to assume the
form of a checklist not only of vocabulary, but of cultural
content as well. As you expand your vocabulary in all directions you will be simultaneously expanding your knowledge
of the culture. As an anthropologist's language improves,
the time spent working on the language will merge imper-
ceptibly into the time spent learning about the culture. Finally, the research that brings an anthropologist to the field
becomes the center of attention. Whatever your goals, as
your language improves, explicit attention to the language
will assume a gradually diminishing proportion of your day,
but the habit of expanding your language skills should become well-enough established to let your language continue
to improve as long as you are in the field.

Before you can reach that point, however, you must learn
to understand just as many words as you can just as quickly
as you can. Until you can instantly recognize several thousand words, you will be regularly forced to interrupt others in
order to ask them to define their words. You can get by with
a somewhat smaller speaking vocabulary, since you can resort to synonyms, circumlocutions, and gestures, but the

number of words you will need, even for speaking, is very large.

If you can learn enough content words for the things you want to talk about and enough function words to provide a verbal matrix within which to set the content words, you will be able to say a great deal even if your grammar remains choppy and your pronunciation strongly accented. With enough words, indeed, you can say almost anything. You may not speak with elegance but you will make yourself understood and you will be able to sustain a conversation. As you stretch your abilities, you will have to cultivate an indifference to the errors that you are bound to make, but plunging ahead with words is, I am convinced, a sensible and practical way to begin to speak. It avoids an awful lot of difficulty.

If all you have is words, of course, your grammar will certainly lack refinement. The prefixes, suffixes, and sound alternations that both complicate a language and make it sound right will still be missing. The solution for broken grammar is time, patience, and a great deal of listening. Even after you begin to work seriously on speaking, continue to devote enough attention to comprehension so that it stays comfortably in advance of your speaking ability. In that way, you will have a growing sense of what the language should sound like, and you will be increasingly able to monitor your own speech without worrying too much about minor grammatical details. In general, I would urge you not to try to use words actively until you understand them quite easily, although this can hardly be a rigid rule. You may, for instance, want to use numbers and courtesy phrases before you can understand them easily, but if your usual practice is to keep comprehension in the lead, you will be able to monitor yourself when you start to use new words actively. When you use words incorrectly they will sound funny and you will gradually learn to correct yourself.

As your listening comprehension advances, you will gradually get a feeling even for the details of grammar, including the complicated rules by which words are built up from their parts. One of the most exciting things that can happen as you get a feeling for how a language is supposed to sound, is to hear yourself using grammatical forms without having self-consciously planned them. That can only happen if you keep comprehension far enough ahead of production to let the patterns of grammar soak in by natural means instead of by rote learning. Be patient, and eventually you will hear little grammatical bits and pieces emerging in your speech, not because you have laboriously planned how to use them, but because they seem to feel right in the context. If you are really trying to use your new language for communication, you will always have to devote most of your conscious attention to the meaning you are trying to convey. In particular, you will have to work very hard to dredge up the most appropriate words from your memory. To the very extent that you are really trying to say something, you will have little chance to worry about proper form. Proper form will come in its time. Be patient. Listen and talk.

Finding Out about Grammar

As comprehension becomes easier and as your productive vocabulary improves, you may finally want to start paying more attention to the grammar. By this time, to be sure, you may not much care. If you can speak and understand freely, the final refinements are largely a matter of pride. If you are getting along all right, you might prefer to let it go and proceed to work on the things you came for. Some field-workers, however, will cling to the idea that it really would be rather nice, in the end, to outgrow the pidgin stage and learn to get things right. At this late stage some more systematic grammatical investigation may finally become useful. I think it would be a great mistake to engage in much grammatical analysis of this sort during your early months in the field.

Grammatical problems boil down to figuring out when to use, and when not to use, some particular "form." A form in this case can be a phrase, a word, or a part of a word, and the choice may be between two alternative forms (e.g., *rode/rided*), between alternative orderings of the same forms (e.g., changes in word order, *did ride/ride did*), or between a form and nothing at all (e.g., *rode/did rode*). What you must do is collect examples that are similar to each other except that some of them use the form in which you are interested while others use an alternative form or nothing at all. You can collect examples either by catching them on the fly as others use them or by deliberately asking for them. When you are uncertain about which form is correct in a particular situation you can ask people for the proper way to say it. If you line up enough examples, both of those accepted as correct and of those rejected, you can search for the conditions that govern the choice among alternatives.

If, for instance, you were trying to learn English, you might want to figure out the rules that English speakers follow when choosing among our various pronunciations of the plural. We usually spell the plural *-s* or *-es* but we pronounce it alternately as /s/, /z/, or /əz/. You would want to collect lists of words that exhibit the alternative pronunciations, and you would want to search among your examples to find what governs the choice among them. Conceivably, your first guess might be that words for living beings require /z/ (*boys, girls, dogs, cows*), while natural objects take /s/ (*rocks, sticks*), and manufactured objects take /əz/ (*houses, buses*). You would very quickly find so many exceptions to this rule, however (*stones, desks, nurses*), that you would be forced to abandon it and to make another guess.

Next you might suppose that the choice among the three variants depends on the syntax of the sentence. Perhaps one form is used in the subject of a sentence, another in the object, and the third in prepositional phrases. Again, however, you would quickly find so many exceptions to this hypothesis that it, too, would have to be abandoned.

Soon you would discover a much more consistent pattern. Barring a few exceptional words (e.g., *men, sheep*) you would find that the form of the plural depends very simply upon the immediately preceding sound, the final sound of the noun to which the plural marker is attached. After a word ending in a vowel or in /b/, /d/, or /g/, for instance, the plural is always pronounced /z/. After /p/, /t/, or /k/, etc., it is pronounced /s/. After /j/, /s/, or /z/ it is pronounced /əz/.

Second language learners sometimes manage to speak understandable (though incorrect) English even though they pronounce most of their plurals alike. Countless others learn to use the alternatives correctly without ever consciously attending to any rule at all. The rule for selecting among plural forms is not one that is crucial for early learners, and it might not be needed later either, but it could be a useful generalization for some learners at a later stage in order to make a final refinement in their language. The hypotheses that I offered and rejected for the rule of plural pronunciation illustrate an important point: the choice among forms can depend upon one of the three things or upon some combination of the three—meaning, syntax, and pronunciation. If you are trying to figure out when to use the *-ed* suffix in English, your most useful generalization will be a semantic rule: *-ed* is used when you want to refer to events in the past. If you are trying to figure out when to say *this* and when to say *that* your most useful first generalization will be that the choice has something to do with the distance of the object, also a semantic rule. Most of your language learning, in fact, will be semantic since most of the time you will be trying to figure out the meaning of words that people use, or to figure out which word will get your own particular meaning across. Sometimes, however, semantic choices get buried among grammatical complexities and you may have to remind yourself that the reason for some alternatives may simply be that they mean different things. Alternative meanings should always be the first explanation that you think about when trying to figure out the difference between alternative forms. As my example of the choice among plurals shows, however, explanations that depend on meaning do not always work.

If the choice among alternative forms (or between a form and nothing) does not depend upon what the speaker is trying to say, it must depend upon either the surrounding sounds (as in the example of different plural forms), or upon the surrounding words (the syntax), or upon some combination of these. If you were trying to figure out the conditions under which the word *did* pops up in English, you would find that explanations based on pronunciation would be of no use at all and that explanations based on meaning would be of only limited use. If you collected enough examples with *did*, however, you would find that a great many of them would be followed by *not* or *-n't*, producing *did not* and *didn't*. By investigating *not* you might then discover that it always follows an auxiliary verb of some sort. You would then realize that when no other auxiliary is available a *did* (or *do*) needs to be supplied. This would give you a partial explanation for the presence of *did*, but you would be left with many other examples and you would have to search further to refine your generalization.

The rules governing the insertion of *did* are primarily syntactic (i.e., they depend upon the relation among the words in the sentences rather than upon either pronunciation or meaning), and a time could come, relatively late in your acquisition of English, when some explicit syntactic generalizations would help you to get the use of *did* sorted out and to use the language correctly. Most such rules are best learned by hearing a great deal of the language and by getting a feel for what "sounds right" (this is, after all, the way all native speakers learn such rules), but foreigners can be given some modest help by having an explicit understanding of them. There is, moreover, considerable intellectual excitement in discovering such rules, and you don't need to deny yourself the fun of exploring them. Just don't imagine that working out rules in the abstract can ever be a substitute for practical experience in listening and talking. You will always learn most by actually using the language, but after you have learned enough to monitor your own speech, some explicit generalizations may give you confidence about talking and help you to work yourself away from your early and inevitable grammatical mistakes.

The very last step in perfecting your grammar is to ask that people correct you when you make an error. This kind of correction is probably essential for the final refinements of linguistic skill. Certain errors do become habitual. Even children learn the final touches of their language with the help of correction, often in the exceedingly effective form of teasing by other children. You won't want much correction in the beginning. It is far too discouraging. This is one good reason not to rely upon a conscientious teacher in the early stages. Teachers may make far more corrections than an early learner can use. But when you have a good enough feel for the language to be able to recognize immediately the correct form as sounding better than your own attempt, you can be helped to edit out your mistakes if people call them to your attention. Always, you have to keep listening. You must keep noting ways in which other people use the language differently from the way you do.

Moving Ahead

One of the unanswerable questions asked of people who return from living abroad is "How long did it take you to learn the language?" Unless you give up completely and stop learning altogether, the only possible answer to this question will be "I was still learning it on my last day there." The more fluent you become, of course, the more you will be able to do with your language. As you come to understand more, and as you begin to use more words yourself, people will probably try to engage you in more complex conversations. You may find yourself subjected to long periods of insistent talk. Struggling for hours with a language in which you are still weak is likely to be one of the most exhausting activities in which you ever engage. You will often be doubtful about the meaning that people are trying to convey to you, and you will face infuriating moments when you simply cannot think of the particular word that will express your meaning. All you can do is keep at it. Gradually, your tongue will loosen.

As your language improves, you will be able to use it in a growing range of practical situations. Some kinds of information can be obtained with relatively limited skill in the language, and you will be able to ask increasingly complex questions about the life and customs of the people you are living among. Anthropologists can collect genealogies while their linguistic skills are still quite limited, although checking your facts at a later time may be desirable so as to make sure that no serious misunderstandings occurred. Technical activities can be demonstrated visually, and the language that is used in connection with the demonstration may be fairly transparent. Every conversation that includes discussion about people's activities, of course, provides an excellent chance for practice with the language. In this way, language learning gradually merges with other kinds of investigations.

Language is the sort of activity in which the more you know the easier it is to learn still more. At first you know so little that you find yourself constantly confused, but with each advance the opportunities for using the language will expand, and this will make it easier to take the next step. It would be a mistake to stop deliberate work on the language just because you are able to begin to use it for obtaining information, however. An adult finds it all too easy to hit a linguistic plateau and stay there. A deliberate attempt to keep vocabulary expanding, to mimic the sounds a little more skillfully, and to refine your grammar should continue as long as you remain in the field.

Keep a notebook for vocabulary handy. When you hear a new word, ask its meaning, jot it down, and learn it well enough to recognize it the next time you hear it. You cannot possibly learn every new word that you hear, but as time goes on and the number of new words gradually declines, you can probably learn an increasing proportion of them. You may always choose to ignore words that seem too esoteric or specialized. You may not have time to learn the name of every subspecies of marsh grass or caterpillar, but you will want to learn to understand, easily, every word that is repeated with any regularity.

When you work hard to increase your comprehension vocabulary, the store of words that you have learned reasonably well will always be supplemented by a penumbra of other words that you understand only in part. This is true even of your native language. Unless you happen to have taken a special interest in horses, you may not have learned the exact meanings of words such as *bridle, fetlock,* or *surrey,* but you probably do know that they have something to do with horses. In order to use a word when speaking, you must know it very well indeed. But in the practical world of language use you are more likely to refine meanings gradually. Starting with a general meaning, you slowly discover the situations in which it is used, and gain a more rounded feeling for its special connotations. As the word becomes consolidated in your memory, and its meaning becomes rounded out, you will finally reach the point where it becomes natural to use it.

Although there is no single point at which you can claim to "know" the language, there are some significant mileposts. An important moment will come when you realize that whenever an unknown word appears you can consistently ask for its meaning and understand the explanation without resorting to a translation. This is the stage that children hit when they are about six years old, and when they insistently ask for the meaning of words that they hear: "What does 'incredible' mean, Daddy?" At some stage you will be able to ask a great many questions of this sort, and be confident of understanding the answers. This is an important stage, because you will have become genuinely emancipated from your own language and you will be able to learn just as easily from a monolingual as from someone who also knows English.

Even after you are able to use the language quite flexibly, I would encourage continued work on comprehension. You should progress from being able to understand someone who speaks to you slowly and carefully to being able to understand someone speaking at a fairly natural speed but who addresses you on a subject with which you are familiar. Keep working on comprehension until you feel that you can understand people of all ages and backgrounds when speaking about a variety of topics and in various styles.

The ultimate test is to be able to follow conversation when people talk to each other in the most rapid and colloquial form of the language, but do not be dismayed if you have not reached this level even after a year or more in the field. The majority of field anthropologists probably never reach this level of skill, and you might take comfort in the realization that this form of language always teeters dangerously on the brink of unintelligibility—even for native speakers. When others are talking rapidly and easily, notice how often someone asks "What did you say?" If native speakers so often fail to understand one another, you should not feel badly about your own difficulties. Still, if you are to participate easily in the life around you, the ability to understand native speakers as fluently as they understand each other is the level of proficiency toward which you should aim.

Even two full years in the field, more time than most anthropologists have, it is not enough to give total fluency in an exotic language. You certainly didn't speak your native language fluently by your second or even your fourth birthday, so don't attribute your less than perfect language ability to the handicaps of adulthood. After two years, an adult should be able to discuss a wider range of topics and use a richer vocabulary than even a five year old, so there are ways in which adults learn much more quickly than children. We imagine that children learn more rapidly than adults because we expect less of them. A five year old speaks perfect five-year-old language. It would be a hopelessly inadequate level for an adult.

Even one year should be enough time to allow you to understand most of the language, at least when it is directed specifically at you, and by using synonyms and circumlocutions creatively you should be able to say whatever you like. You will continue to make many grammatical mistakes and you will pronounce some things badly, but you will be communicating, and you will be in much closer contact with the life around you than would ever be possible if your knowledge had to be filtered through an interpreter. You will be able to learn about the culture far more rapidly and acquire a more profound understanding of your surroundings. You will have become your own interpreter. You will not have turned over that crucial part of your job to someone else. And, by no means least important, you will have had an awful lot more fun.

Notes

1. Theoretical support for the priority of comprehension, and reports of pedagogical experiments that emphasize comprehension, will be found in Harris Winitz, *The Comprehension Approach to Foreign Language Instruction* (Rowley, Mass.: Newbury House Press, 1981), and in my own *Sounding Right* (Rowley, Mass.: Newbury House Press, 1982).
2. The Keyword method has been described in a number of articles. See, for instance, Joel R. Levin, "Assessing the Classroom Potential of the Keyword Method," *Journal of Educational Psychology* 71:583–94 (1979), and R. Merry, "The Keyword Method and Children's Vocabulary Learning in the Classroom," *British Journal of Educational Psychology* 50(2): 23–36.
3. Henry Kučera and W. Nelson Francis, *Computational Analysis of Present-Day American English* (Providence, R.I.: Brown University Press, 1967). Hartvig Dahl, *Word Frequencies of Spoken American English* (Detroit: Gale Research Company, 1979).
4. Surprisingly little systematic research has been done to test this widespread impression, but see Peter Strevens, *New Orientations in the Teaching of English* (Oxford: Oxford University Press, 1977), 28ff., and John J. Deveny and J. C. Bockout, "The Intensive Language Course: Toward a Successful Approach," *Foreign Language Annals,* 1976, pp. 58–64.
5. This is similar to the "Total Physical Response" pioneered by James Asher and described in his book *Learning Another Language Through Actions* (Los Gatos, Calif.: Sky Oaks Publications, 1977).

Appendixes

Appendix 1
Learning Monolingually

In the body of this work, I have assumed that you will be able to find someone who speaks a contact language and whose knowledge you can exploit in order to speed up the early stages of your own learning. Only on rare occasions today is a field-worker forced to learn from monolinguals. Even when you can obtain some help from bilinguals, however, you will sometimes find yourself wanting to talk with monolinguals and you will want to make such situations as productive as possible. In fact, if it is at all possible, you should now and then deliberately cut yourself off from consultants who speak English in order to avoid becoming too dependent upon them. In this section I offer a few hints about how to proceed monolingually.

First, the most essential ingredient of the monolingual method is the nonverbal, or extralinguistic, context. Since you have no other language to fall back on when trying to figure out what a word, phrase, or sentence means, you are absolutely dependent upon the nonverbal context to give the language its meaning. You have little choice but to start by pointing at things. Keep pointing and looking quizzical until people get the idea that you want the names for all those things. Careful notes are particularly important with this method, since it is far more difficult than with a bilingual consultant to go back and check up on what you have heard. If you are careful to take good notes as you go along, it may be worthwhile to record some sessions in which you elicit words and phrases so that you can listen to them later and fix what you have heard in your memory. Recordings will be of little use without very careful notes, however. Without gestures or the context of the conversation, it is very difficult to reconstruct the meaning of recordings unless the notes are full and clear.

Once people realize that you want names for the things that you point to, it is almost too easy to go on collecting dozens and hundreds of names. Before you get bogged down, you will want to move on to other classes of words. You can get words for body parts and then, by pointing first to your own eyes, then to your consultants eyes, and then to someone else's eyes you should be able to get possessive words: *my eyes, your eyes, our eyes.* By pointing at closer and more distant examples of similar objects, words for *this* and *that* are likely to pop out. You can point to things that are alike except for such qualities as size or color and begin to get the descriptive adjectives that distinguish them. You can perform simple actions like walking, sitting down, standing up, or eating and get people to give you the words for these activities. When these words are used with different people, you should be able to elicit pronouns that describe who is performing the actions. You can hand objects around and get phrases for *I give you the stick,* etc.

Step-by-step, you can work your way up to such complex sentences as *The little rock is on top of these two sheets of paper,* or *You and I are walking toward that pig by the big house.* These may not be the sentences you most urgently need, but they will give you a good start. The more words you can learn from such sentences, the better you will be able to isolate and focus upon the remaining words. To make this effort successful, you need cooperation, and you must hope to find yourself among people who think that it is more fun than trouble to help a struggling outsider. Your smiles, your attention to gestures of courtesy, your willingness to accept ridicule, all become crucially important.

This method is necessarily slower than the bilingual method, and it becomes even more crucial to catch things when they appear and to try to learn them efficiently so you will be able to build up your ability to understand just as quickly as possible. In order to elicit language in this way, you will have to use a good deal of the language yourself. You will have to try out sentences and accept the corrections that people offer. Occasionally you may even want to make deliberate mistakes so as to receive their corrections and learn how something really ought to be said. You may learn the words for *my* and *your* by pointing to different people's body parts. Then you can experiment by using the same words along with the word for *walk: my walk, your walk.* Perhaps you will come close enough to the correct phrases to let someone understand what you are groping for, and offer corrections: *I walk* and *you walk.*

By manipulating objects and performing actions with your body you can elicit language to describe a wider and wider range of activities. If you want to make rapid progress you have to be very attentive and snatch anything that happens to come your way. Usually you can convey the idea of a question by pointing at something, and looking quizzical. In most languages (but not quite all!) a rising intonation suggests a question. When the person with whom you are speaking uses an unknown word in a situation that suggests its meaning, take a guess and grab it. Try it out in situations where you can test it to see if it really means what it seems to mean. Sooner or later you are likely to hear words, perhaps accompanied by gestures, that seem, from the context, to mean such things as *no, yes, what?, I don't know.* Grab them. Make notes. If you suspect that a particular word means *no* you can deliberately call something by its wrong name and see whether you can get someone to say *no* again. You have to keep the context simple enough to let it suggest plausible meanings.

You will have to start with quite short utterances, but you will quickly progress to longer and longer sequences. You have to memorize as much as you can as quickly as you can, so that you can focus your attention on the remainder. Much more than in the bilingual method you have to rely upon seizing whatever happens to come your way. You will have a more difficult time eliciting the specific words you need. Since you cannot ask "How do you say 'terrible' in your language?" you have to wait until a word is used in a situation where it seems to mean *terrible.* When this happens, it is important to note the word right away so that you can recognize it the next time it appears and use it yourself when you need it.

Some areas of meaning are relatively accessible. Position, location, and the relation of objects in space can be elicited quite easily because you can manipulate objects and place them in spatial relation to each other. Time relationships are far more difficult. Children learning their first language sometimes have great trouble sorting out the meaning of words like *yesterday* and *tomorrow.* It is not possible to point to *tomorrow,* and it is very difficult to define such a word by using other words. You may face a similar problem with words like *tomorrow,* but at least you do have the knowledge that a language is likely to have such words, and when someone uses a sentence that seems to be describing a future event, you can make a note of it and wait to see when it happens.

Abstract words are the most difficult. Words like *try, decide, hope,* and *spirit* may cause serious problems. When you begin to hear what seems to be a word used repeatedly but in puzzling situations, focus on it, note its contexts, and try to abstract its usage. You will want to work toward controlling enough vocabulary so that it will begin to be possible for people to use the words you already know to give you definitions of other words that you don't yet know. You have to start by inferring meaning from the nonverbal context, but later you will be able to add new words by having the meanings defined by old familiar words. This is an important step, but it is not likely to come for several months.

Building up the language careful step by careful step is crucial. No single utterance can contain too much that is new, or you will be unable to understand it. You will have no way of sorting out the unknowns. Nevertheless, if you are alert, if you grab what other people say and seize your opportunities, you can work steadily toward a wider and wider knowledge of the language. People will very quickly start using full sentences that exhibit all the grammatical apparatus of the language. You will have no way of untangling this apparatus at first but will have to guess. Try to use sentences that sound right even if you don't know what all the parts mean and accept corrections that are offered. Always notice the context.

If you need to learn your language monolingually, you can, at least, take comfort in the knowledge that your predicament does force you to do a number of helpful things. Being unable to fall back upon a contact language, you are forced to practice your new language in every sort of situation. You will not be tempted to lean on an English-speaking consultant or interpreter. It can be terribly embarrassing to speak broken Ashanti to someone who speaks fine English. Too much English in your surroundings can fatally inhibit your ability to get practice with your new language. In a monolingual situation you are forced to overcome your own embarrassment. The urgency with which the language impinges upon you may more than compensate for the apparent disadvantages of lacking the help of a bilingual consultant.

Appendix 2
Literary and National Languages

I have written this book primarily for those who need to learn a language that has neither teachers nor classes nor books. For such a language, learners cannot rely on others but must take the initiative themselves. My suggestions, however, may also have relevance even for those who want to learn a more widely spoken, or more literary language. If you find yourself living in Bangkok or Warsaw or Buenos Aires and if you want to learn Thai or Polish or Spanish, your problems will hardly be identical to those of a jungle anthropologist, but neither will they be entirely different.

Living in a city and working among well-educated people puts special barriers in the way of English speakers. When others are accustomed to speaking English with foreigners, they do not adjust easily to the possibility that a foreigner might be able to speak their language. Where standards of correctness are clearly defined, people may be reluctant to accept the broken efforts of an educated visitor. They will not expect educated people to speak like that, and a visitor may have to reach a rather advanced level before using the new language stops being an acute embarrassment. It is all too easy for English speakers to live for many years in a foreign capital without ever learning more than a few words of the local language. On the other hand, the fact that so few English speakers make any serious attempt to learn the language means that the efforts of the odd individual who gives it a real try are often warmly welcomed.

If I were living in a foreign city, I would try not to spend all my time among the educated elite who speak fine English, but I would, when possible, deliberately seek out monolinguals. I would try to talk to my neighbor's children. I would do my own marketing. If I were hiring a cook I would choose someone who spoke no English so that I would bring the language insistently into my own home. If I were hiring a tutor I would choose a high school student who would follow my lead, rather than a professional teacher who would feel he had not done his job until he had corrected my every mistake, and who might even push me toward an artificially elitist or literary form of the language.

Even if the language you want to learn is equipped with grammars, dictionaries, and professional teachers, I would counsel a greater attention to comprehension than has been typical of a good deal of formal language instruction. An emphasis upon comprehension circumvents some of the special problems of the urban and educated milieu. In Bangkok, as in the wilds of New Guinea, you should be able to persuade a consultant to help you with understanding. Just as in more remote areas, you can make recordings of words and sentences and replay them until you can understand them easily. You can start with isolated words and sentences, move on to connected discourse, and then to dialogues. You can work hard to build up your receptive vocabulary. None of this need be different from learning an unwritten language.

Unlike tribal languages, however, national languages are used in writing, the radio, television, and the movies, and these can be both a help and a burden. When a language uses the Roman alphabet, reading allows an easy and obvious means of expanding your linguistic experience, but literary languages are often complicated by elaborate formal styles that can add greatly to your difficulties. A writing system that is quite different from your own can pose so many extra problems that it may, at first, be more work than it is worth, but the very existence of a writing system means that you will be cut off from some areas of life if you do not learn to read. Illiteracy is no handicap among other illiterates but it becomes a handicap in a society where much of daily information is passed by writing. This means that a literate language can involve the extra work of learning to read.

With a literate language you will, on the other hand, be able to find dictionaries, grammatical descriptions, and texts that are designed to instruct foreigners. If you can use the writing system, bilingual dictionaries are the most useful of the three, but even if you cannot, the chances are good that you can find some sort of word list or short dictionary with words transliterated into the Roman alphabet. A sketch of general grammatical patterns can be helpful, but grammatical descriptions have a way of becoming so technical or so filled with minutiae that the beginner can find them more discouraging than useful. A good rule of thumb is the shorter the grammatical description the better. That way you can get an overview of what is really important without getting lost in exceptions or special cases. Texts that are specifically designed to teach the spoken language, unfortunately, almost always on focus on production rather than comprehension. Some texts even manage to convey the impression that getting out a grammatically elegant sentence is essential but almost impossibly difficult. Techniques for survival, which is what you need, can be lost in a quest for the subjunctive. Still, you should certainly look for and take advantage of practical pedagogical materials. They can save you a great deal of anguish, and you should be able to find materials that are useful for reference, even if you do not want to work your way systematically through their lessons.

Rather than working through the formal lessons of a textbook, you may find it more useful to find a book that has been translated so that you can use the English version as a "pony" to help you with the foreign version. A dictionary is essential too, but a translation will help you in many places where even a dictionary will fail, since a translation will give you the meaning not only of words, but of constructions as well. It is most interesting to use a book originally written in your new language along with an English translation since this will give you a view of the new culture as well as of the language, but it may be easier, at first, to use a book that has been translated *into* your new language. Translators almost always use a narrower range of vocabulary than do original authors and thus make the translation easier for a new learner. Agatha Christie mysteries, for instance, have been translated into dozens of languages. If you can read the translation while using the original as a handy reference, you may have a relatively easy way to begin your literary adventures. You can, of course, start with children's books or with a book of graded readings for foreigners, but the contents are likely to be insipid and the added interest of adult material may make the extra difficulties a small price to pay. With a translation and a dictionary it is possible even for a relative beginner to work, slowly to be sure, through quite difficult material.

You can make reading both easier and more useful if you have a speaker of the language read the text that you plan to work on into a tape recorder. If you listen and read at the same time, the spoken and written versions will support each other, and understanding will be easier than with either version alone. The spoken form will save you from the worst pronunciation distortions that will come if you have only the writing, and hearing the words should help them to stick in your mind. In addition, the intonation of the spoken language, as given by someone who reads aloud fluently, will provide clues to the grammatical structure. Even while your language is still rudimentary, you will be able to hear the patterns of emphasis and the way words are grouped into phrases. This will help you understand what is on the page. At the same time, the written version will give the words in their fully spelled form, without the reductions, contractions, and abbreviations that make fast spoken language so difficult. Written words also come nicely isolated by white spaces so that you can find them in a dictionary.

Radio, television, and the movies are less valuable than they might seem. The language of these media goes by so quickly that it is impossible for the beginner to catch the meaning. There is no way to slow speakers down and, even worse, there is no easy way to get explanations for parts that are missed. You may find it helpful to tape-record short passages from the radio and listen to them repeatedly, but listening several times to five or ten minutes of a radio broadcast is likely to build up your comprehension more effectively than the same amount of time spent listening to a long passage just once. If you can use a dictionary, you may occasionally be able to look up a word that you hear on your recording, but many words will surely fly by so quickly that you cannot possibly guess their spelling. It is more useful to have a friend go over a recording carefully with you and explain the meanings of unfamiliar words and phrases.

Radio recordings are better than recordings of television

programs because radio talk is more continuous and radio language must be used in ways that do not depend upon the visible context. Some subjects are easier than others. Weather reports tend to be quite easy since they are short and use a very stereotyped vocabulary. International news everywhere follows a similar style, and your familiarity with the subject matter will ease your comprehension. Drama and sports are likely to be considerably more difficult, but you can work your way toward understanding them.

Classes in the language can be very useful in keeping you motivated and in giving you a regular opportunity to practice. If, in addition, you are willing to take a good deal of initiative yourself, just as you would be forced to do in a more remote field situation, and if you can resist the efforts of some teachers to correct every mistake or to burden you with an overly elegant or literary form of the language, you should find regular classes a useful addition to your studies. Remember, however, to mimic the pronunciation of native speakers, not that of your classmates, and do not fool yourself into imagining that a couple of hours a week in class can ever be a substitute for lots of individual effort outside of class.

In the end, the strategy for learning a literary language in an urban setting is not really so different from that of learning an unwritten language in the countryside. You must seek opportunities, first to listen to the language and then to practice it, in an ever-expanding range of activities. As with any language, the more you know, the easier it is to learn still more. And as with any language, knowledge opens up worlds from which you would otherwise be firmly excluded.